Esther

Five Feasts and the
Fingerprints of God

Esther

Five Feasts and the Fingerprints of God

by

Dr. Bo Wagner

Word of His Mouth Publishers
Mooresboro, NC

All Scripture quotations are taken from the **King James Version** of the Bible.

ISBN: 978-0-9856042-2-6
Printed in the United States of America
©2012 Dr. Bo Wagner (Robert Arthur Wagner)

Word of His Mouth Publishers
PO Box 256
Mooresboro, NC 28114

Table of Content

Dedication

This book is about a queen, an amazing lady that seemed to come out of nowhere and propel those around her to greatness. It is fitting then that I dedicate this book to my wife, my queen, who is every bit as amazing as Esther herself. When I was in my early twenties, Dana Sessions dropped into my life seemingly out of nowhere. But in reality, she was directed by God into my life just as Esther was directed into the life of Ahasuerus. I had saved myself for a special woman, waited, prayed, and God answered that prayer in the greatest way possible! We met in church as her missionary father traveled on deputation. From the moment I saw her, I knew she was the one that God had planned for me from before the dawn of time. We met that night, and I asked her out. She gave me ten reasons why she could not go, and I gave her eleven why she could. When she ran out of reasons, we went out, and the rest is history. We were married 11 months later. This queen of mine then followed me into the ministry, which has been every bit as adventurous (and at times, almost as dangerous) as the events of the book of Esther. She helped me start a church from nothing. She crawled up on the church roof with me to help me finish the shingles before the rain started. She painted, mopped, mowed, trimmed, wired, and framed right alongside me. Then on Sunday, she put on her fanciest, painted her nails, played the piano, and smiled a warm smile for everyone. She has served as the church secretary since the first year. She has physically chased down a thief trying to steal the church children's change jug (amazing lady, this wife of mine!) She makes hospitals visits with me, knocks on doors, edits books, and does the church I.T. work. She has produced and is raising three beautiful children for me. She is well bred, well educated, brilliant, beautiful, firm, decisive, talented, and fun to be around. With this queen at my side, I am pretty well equipped to face the Hamans of this world. I love you, Sweetheart, and this book is for you.

Introduction

She held her breath, hoping for the best. If the last few years had been a whirlwind, the last few days had been a category five hurricane in her life. She thought back to the time when she along with everyone else had heard the shocking news; Queen Vashti had been removed and divorced. That set off a flurry of activity. A beauty pageant was called as a way of deciding upon a new queen. When the dust had settled, Esther herself, against all odds, was the new queen of the Persian Empire. Who could have imagined a Jewess in such a position! Wisely, she had observed the command of old Mordecai not to tell anyone of her race. Since the days of the Pharaohs, God's people had always managed to be singled out for ill-treatment by whoever was in power. Not telling anyone of her heritage gave her a measure of protection that she, even as the queen, would need.

Things had been, oh, so good these last few years. She enjoyed a life of luxury that no Jew since the time of Solomon could have imagined.

But then her world fell apart and the gale force winds began to blow. Her own husband's second in command, a twisted old man named Haman, had managed to pass a law allowing for all of the Jews in the empire to be killed! This law was signed with her husband's own ring, showing how much confidence the king had in Haman. This put Esther in a very bad position. She had not been called into her husband's presence for thirty days, and to come before him unannounced could mean her death. Nevertheless, she came. He extended the golden scepter to her, granting her permission to be there. Quickly she asked for the king and Haman to come to a banquet she had prepared for them, promising to tell him what she desired. At that banquet, she added a layer of mystery by coming within a breath of stating her request and then promising to tell him at tomorrow's banquet if he and Haman would come.

Tomorrow came and so did the king and Haman. Now, here she was, having just pointed out Haman, whom she called "this wicked Haman," as a would-be mass murderer of her and her people. Everything now hung in the balance. Who would the king believe? Someone was going to die that day, of this she was sure. But would it be Haman's neck or her own in the noose?

Chapter 1

The Boys Have Their Heads Together, Trouble Can't Be Far Away

Esther 1:1 *Now it came to pass in the days of Ahasuerus, (this is Ahasuerus which reigned, from India even unto Ethiopia, over an hundred and seven and twenty provinces:) 2 That in those days, when the king Ahasuerus sat on the throne of his kingdom, which was in Shushan the palace, 3 In the third year of his reign, he made a feast unto all his princes and his servants; the power of Persia and Media, the nobles and princes of the provinces, being before him: 4 When he shewed the riches of his glorious kingdom and the honour of his excellent majesty many days, even an hundred and fourscore days. 5 And when these days were expired, the king made a feast unto all the people that were present in Shushan the palace, both unto great and small, seven days, in the court of the garden of the king's palace; 6 Where were white, green, and blue, hangings, fastened with cords of fine linen and purple to silver rings and pillars of marble: the beds were of gold and silver, upon a pavement of red, and blue, and white, and black, marble. 7 And they gave them drink in vessels of gold, (the vessels being diverse one* *from another,) and royal wine in abundance, according to the state of the king.* **8** *And the drinking was according to the law; none did compel: for so the king had appointed to all the officers of his house, that they should do according to every man's pleasure.* **9** *Also Vashti the queen made a feast for the women in the royal house which belonged to king Ahasuerus.* **10** *On the seventh day, when the heart of the king was merry with wine, he commanded Mehuman, Biztha, Harbona, Bigtha, and Abagtha, Zethar, and Carcas, the seven chamberlains that served in the presence of Ahasuerus the king,* **11** *To bring Vashti the queen before the king with the crown royal, to shew the people and the princes her beauty: for she was fair to look on.* **12** *But the queen Vashti refused to come at the king's commandment by his chamberlains: therefore was the king very wroth, and his anger burned in him.* **13** *Then the king said to the wise men, which knew the times, (for so was the king's manner toward all that knew law and judgment:* **14** *And the next unto him was Carshena, Shethar, Admatha, Tarshish, Meres, Marsena, and Memucan, the seven princes of Persia and Media, which saw the king's face, and which sat the first in the kingdom;)* **15** *What shall we do unto the queen Vashti according to law, because she hath not performed the commandment of the king Ahasuerus by the chamberlains?* **16** *And Memucan answered before the king and the princes, Vashti the queen hath not done wrong to the king only, but also to all the princes, and to all the people that are in all the provinces of the king Ahasuerus.* **17** *For this deed of the queen shall come abroad unto all women, so that they shall despise their husbands in their eyes, when it shall be reported, The king Ahasuerus commanded Vashti the queen to* *be brought in before him, but she came not.* **18** *Likewise shall the ladies of Persia and Media say this day unto all the king's princes, which have heard of the deed of the queen. Thus shall there arise too much contempt and wrath.* **19** *If it please the king, let there go a royal commandment from him, and let it be written among the laws of the Persians and the Medes, that it be not altered, That Vashti come no more before king Ahasuerus; and let the king give her royal estate unto another that is better than she.* **20** *And when the king's decree which he shall make shall be published throughout all his empire, (for it is great,) all the wives shall give to their husbands honour, both to great and small.* **21** *And the saying pleased the king and the princes; and the king did according to the word of Memucan:* **22** *For he sent letters into all the king's provinces, into every province according to the writing thereof, and to every people after their language, that every man should bear rule in his own house, and that it should be published according to the language of every people.*

In 606 B.C., over 2600 years ago, the southern kingdom of Israel, known as Judah, was taken into captivity in Babylon. The northern kingdom, still called by the name Israel, had been taken captive by Assyria years before. Originally all of the twelve tribes were together as one nation, but there had been a civil war in the days of Rehoboam, the son of Solomon, the son of David, and the nation had been spilt in two. Now both were gone. The ten northern tribes, Israel, are never shown as having a wholesale return to their homeland. A few came back, but for the most part they have not been a large presence either in Scripture or in history. The Bible does make it clear, though, that one day they will be again. But the history of the two southern tribes, Judah, is followed closely through the Scriptures. When you read the book of Daniel you are reading about Judah and about the seventy year captivity in Babylon as seen through the eyes of four Hebrew princes. Their names were Daniel, Hananiah, Azariah, and Mishael. You most likely remember those last three by the names the Babylonians gave them: Shadrach, Meshach, and Abednego. When you read the book of Ezra you are reading about some Jews from the captivity who were allowed to go back to Judah eighty years after captivity was ended to rebuild the temple in Jerusalem. When you read the book of Nehemiah you are reading about some Jews who were allowed to go and rebuild the walls of Jerusalem 93 years after the captivity was over. You see, after having been in Babylon for seventy years in captivity, not everyone wanted to go back home when it was over. Most of them had been born in Babylon; that was home to them! And that is where the book of Esther comes into play. Esther is about God's people who were still living in what used to be Chaldaea with the capital city of Babylon but was now known as Persia (modern day Iran) with its capital city of Shushan. Babylon had fallen to the Medes and the Persians, and the Persian Empire quickly became the most powerful empire then on Earth. Thousands and thousands of Jews still lived there. Some had gone home, most had stayed behind, but the God that loved them was still the same.

Esther is a unique book, not just in the fact that it is one of only two books in the Bible named after a woman. It is more unique than that in that it is the only book in the Bible where the name of God is not mentioned! It is often criticized for that, but unjustly so. You see, though the name of God is not mentioned, His fingerprints are everywhere. Evidence of Him watching over His people is everywhere. Things happen throughout the book that only He could have done.

We are going to go through the book of Esther together. Everything *seen* in this book revolves around five feasts. Everything *unseen* in this book revolves around the fingerprints of God.

There Was a Feast of Wine

Esther 1:1 *Now it came to pass in the days of Ahasuerus, (this is Ahasuerus which reigned, from India even unto Ethiopia, over an hundred and seven and twenty provinces:) 2 That in those days, when the king Ahasuerus sat on the throne of his kingdom, which was in Shushan the palace, 3 In the third year of his reign, he made a feast unto all his princes and his servants; the power of Persia and Media, the nobles and princes of the provinces, being before him: 4 When he shewed the riches of his glorious kingdom and the honour of his excellent majesty many days, even an hundred and fourscore days.*

The book of Esther begins by introducing us to a king, a man by the name of Ahasuerus. The name he is more commonly known by to historians is Xerxes.[1] Please, allow me to tell you just a bit about him, because once you know what kind of a man he was, the things you read about in the book of Esther will make much more sense.

Xerxes was a man who had both a soft side and a brutally hard side. On the soft side, he loved luxury; he loved living the good life. He was a womanizer even though the law of the Medes and Persians forbade it.

13

On the brutally hard side, he was a bloodthirsty and merciless tyrant and a man with an amazingly hot temper. When his army was marching toward Greece, a man named Pythius, who had given Xerxes a huge amount of money and supplies and to whom Xerxes had pledged undying friendship, asked a reasonable request. He had five sons and all were in Xerxes army. He asked if just one of them could stay home to take care of him and his wife in their old age. Xerxes flew into a rage. He agreed to leave that one son behind... in two pieces. He had his army cut the boy in half and then marched his entire army between those two pieces as they left town, with a father and mother left behind sobbing over their loss.

That doesn't begin to tell the full tale of his temper and cruelty. He also had the builders of the bridge over the Hellespont beheaded because a massive storm destroyed the bridge.[2]

This is the Ahasuerus we are reading about in the first verse of the book of Esther. Now you understand why he so calmly agreed to the slaughter of hundreds of thousands of his subjects when Haman suggested it!

In verse three we are told that Ahasuerus was in the third year of his reign. He was about to embark on a massive military campaign against the Greeks. In order to get everyone fired up, he basically held a giant pep rally, 180 days worth, with all the free booze his people could want.

There were princes, nobles, royal servants, all the bigwigs, everybody who was anybody was there at the half a year long party.

Esther 1:5 *And when these days were expired, the king made a feast unto all the people that were present in Shushan* *the palace, both unto great and small, seven days, in the court of the garden of the king's palace; 6 Where were white, green, and blue, hangings, fastened with cords of fine linen and purple to silver rings and pillars of marble: the beds were of gold and silver, upon a pavement of red, and blue, and white, and black, marble.*

When the 180 day party for the important people had been concluded, Ahasuerus decided to add another seven days onto it and to throw open the doors for anyone in the palace, even the "unimportant" people. So you have 187 days of a "pat me on the back party" thrown by this self-centered king; 187 days of a pep rally getting ready for war against Greece. The entire 187 days of this feast centered around booze and beds. Verse six mentions the beds, which were luxurious couches for all the guests to recline on while they were getting plastered. We can't have drunks trying to do anything difficult like stand up, now can we?

Esther 1:7 *And they gave them drink in vessels of gold, (the vessels being diverse one from another,) and royal wine in abundance, according to the state of the king. 8 And the drinking was according to the law; none did compel: for so the king had appointed to all the officers of his house, that they should do according to every man's pleasure.*

Everything Ahasuerus did at this long party was to show off. He didn't have them drinking out of paper cups; he had them drinking out of golden vessels. This was designed to send a message: *Look at us! Look how great we are! No one can beat us!* Ahasuerus was going to find out the hard way that being rich does not equal success in battle.

But, for that moment, everything was perfect for him and his people. There were all the booze anyone could want, golden cups from which to drink, and according to verse eight, the drinking was *"according to the law; none did compel... everyone did according to his pleasure."*

Now that is an odd set of phrases; we should examine what they mean. Among the ancients there was a proverb: *Drink or be gone.* It meant that there was a person at each table who would decide whether there was another round or not, and if he decided there was, everyone there had to participate.[3] Some would feel they had drunk to much; some would feel they had drunk too little. But Ahasuerus decided to remove all restrictions. If a person wanted to just have a few, he theoretically could do so. If a person wanted to get absolutely plastered, he could do so and no one would tell him he had too much. But who in that setting is going to want to be the one not hoisting one more toast to Xerxes, the guy with the nasty temper and the habit of killing people? So what has been produced is a setting in which a whole lot of people spent more than half a year drunk out of their minds.

Yes, sir, the boys are having quite a time. But it is at this point that the girls began to be mentioned:

Esther 1:9 *Also Vashti the queen made a feast for the women in the royal house which belonged to king Ahasuerus.*

Please, pay attention to the fact that these were two separate feasts being held at the same time but being held in separate places. That is very important. You see, in Oriental society, especially back then, the men and women did not mingle at social occasions. It was considered very inappropriate.[4] [5] John Wesley said, "This was the common

16

custom of the Persians, that men and women did not feast together."[6]

So the men were in one place holding their feast; the ladies were in another place holding theirs. The ladies feast was being held by the queen, a woman named Vashti. Her name means *Beautiful*.[7] It was probably not her birth name. When people came to stay in the court of the king their names were normally changed. You remember in the book of Daniel that Daniel, Hananiah, Azariah, and Mishael, had their names changed to Belteshazzar, Shadrach, Meshach, and Abednego. In the next chapter of Esther you will find out that Esther's original name was Hadasssah. This tells us that Vashti was gorgeous. The king or his advisors gave her the name "Beautiful."

So here is what we have so far: a hot tempered king is throwing a 187 day drunken pep-rally party before going off to war, while his beautiful wife is also throwing a party in separate quarters.

There Was a Foul Demand

Esther 1:10 *On the seventh day, when the heart of the king was merry with wine, he commanded Mehuman, Biztha, Harbona, Bigtha, and Abagtha, Zethar, and Carcas, the seven chamberlains that served in the presence of Ahasuerus the king,* **11** *To bring Vashti the queen before the king with the crown royal, to shew the people and the princes her beauty: for she was fair to look on.*

I want you to pay attention to those words, "merry with wine." Let me convert those three words into a one-word definition: drunk. Ahasuerus was out of his mind, stoned

17

drunk. And in that drunken condition, he made a demand that was wrong for him to make, and I mean wrong in every way.

His demand was that Vashti come parade her beauty before all of those leering, drunken men. I have said, and I stand by my statement, that it was wrong in every way. Now, please, allow me to tell you how it was wrong in every way.

It was wrong morally, this one should be obvious to everyone.

Matthew 5:28 *But I say unto you, That whosoever looketh on a woman to lust after her hath committed adultery with her already in his heart.*

It was wrong maritally to demand that a wife arouse the lust of men to whom she was not married and to have that demand made by her own husband! According to Ephesians 5 a husband is to work to present his wife to himself, not to others!

It was also wrong culturally. The custom of the Persians did not allow for a woman to appear in public.[8]

It was wrong due to their royal station as well. According to Persian customs, the queen, even more than the wives of other men, was secluded from the public gaze.[9]

In every way imaginable what Ahasuerus asked was dead wrong. Vashti knew it, and she responded accordingly.

Esther 1:12 *But the queen Vashti refused to come at the king's commandment by his chamberlains: therefore was the king very wroth, and his anger burned in him.*

No one except God has the right to be obeyed at all times no matter what. My wife is commanded to obey me as her husband, but if I tell her that I have decided that our entire family is going to become Satanists, she better obey God instead of me.

We are commanded to obey government, but if government tells us we cannot speak of Jesus, we better obey God rather than government.

Members are commanded to obey their pastor, but if a pastor ever decides that polygamy is acceptable and that all the men need to have three or four wives, they better obey God rather than the pastor.

Children are commanded to obey their parents, but if their parents tell them to convert from Christianity to Islam, they better obey God rather than their parents.

Years ago I listened to a foolish woman Bible teacher on the radio tell another woman that she had to go downtown and watch pornography with her husband because he demanded it. That "Dear One" is an idiot.

The Bible puts it this way:

Acts 5:29 *Then Peter and the other apostles answered and said, We ought to obey God rather than men.*

Now, please, pay very careful attention. This does not mean that any of us are to be looking for an excuse to disobey those in authority over us. Vashti wasn't looking for an excuse to disobey Ahasuerus; this thing got thrust upon her out of nowhere. If you as wives or children or members of a church or U.S. citizens are *looking* for an excuse to disobey husband or parents or pastor or government then your heart is not right. But if you are forced to choose between God and man and you choose man, your heart isn't right then either!

Vashti did right in refusing that foul request. Please understand, she knew full well that she may be tortured and killed because of it. She was willing to do right no matter what the cost. God give us more people just like that!

There Was a Foolish King

Esther 1:13 *Then the king said to the wise men, which knew the times, (for so was the king's manner toward all that knew law and judgment:* **14** *And the next unto him was Carshena, Shethar, Admatha, Tarshish, Meres, Marsena, and Memucan, the seven princes of Persia and Media, which saw the king's face, and which sat the first in the kingdom;)* **15** *What shall we do unto the queen Vashti according to law, because she hath not performed the commandment of the king Ahasuerus by the chamberlains?*

May I remind you, please, of the condition of these seven geniuses? All of them had spent 187 days at the drinking party. They reeked of booze, their eyes were red, their speech slurred, they were toasted. These are the men that the king turned to for guidance!

It takes a very foolish man to turn to drunken buddies for guidance on his marriage or anything else for that matter. It takes a foolish person, man or woman, to turn to any wrong person or persons for guidance. People are thinking of getting out of church, so instead of going to someone who has been faithful for 30 years, they go ask the people who have all the stability of a rabid squirrel what they think. A lady is thinking of leaving her husband, so she asks the gal at work who is on husband number five what she thinks. A guy is mad because his wife wants him to spend time with her rather than spend hours every night playing video games like he is still a kid, so he goes for counsel to the guys he plays Modern Warfare with every night and asks what they think. You better be very careful whom you choose as counselors! Do you know a good way to guide your decision? Ask yourself, "Am I really looking for good counsel, or am I looking to see who I can find to agree with the decision I have already made?"

Ahasuerus turned to his drunken hired hands and asked what they thought should be done. Predictably, he got an answer that only brain-dead drunks could ever come up with:

Esther 1:16 *And Memucan answered before the king and the princes, Vashti the queen hath not done wrong to the king only, but also to all the princes, and to all the people that are in all the provinces of the king Ahasuerus. 17 For this deed of the queen shall come abroad unto all women, so that they shall despise their husbands in their eyes, when it shall be reported, The king Ahasuerus commanded Vashti the queen to be brought in before him, but she came not. 18 Likewise shall the ladies of Persia and Media say this day unto all the king's princes, which have heard of the deed of the queen. Thus shall there arise too much contempt and wrath. 19 If it please the king, let there go a royal commandment from him, and let it be written among the laws of the Persians and the Medes, that it be not altered, That Vashti come no more before king Ahasuerus; and let the king give her royal estate unto another that is better than she.*

Notice, please, something that Memucan does as he begins to tell what should happen to Vashti. There is a word that he uses five times in three verses:

Esther 1:16 *And Memucan answered before the king and the princes, Vashti the queen hath not done wrong to the king only, but also to **all** the princes, and to **all** the people that* *are in **all** the provinces of the king Ahasuerus. **17** For this deed of the queen shall come abroad unto **all** women, so that they shall despise their husbands in their eyes, when it shall be reported, The king Ahasuerus commanded Vashti the queen to be brought in before him, but she came not. **18** Likewise shall the ladies of Persia and Media say this day unto **all** the king's princes, which have heard of the deed of the queen. Thus shall there arise too much contempt and wrath.*

May I paraphrase? "King, you gots to do somethin'. Every single woman in the whole wide world is gonna hear what Vashti did, and every one of those women in every country in the whole wide world is gonna git all high and mighty aginst every one of their husbands!"

Don't you think that is just a bit melodramatic? It takes drunken men to come up with something so over the top as that. The truth is, if Ahasuerus had just let it go, it would have probably been forgotten. Everyone was drunk anyway! How much do you think they were going to remember about all of this once they sobered up? But by publishing it all around the world, which he literally did, everybody in the world did find out about it! The reaction to the problem caused far more trouble than the problem itself.

Notice also, though, the self-serving rationale behind what Memucan said. According to verse fourteen, he was one of those "princes" that he spoke of, whose wives were likely to "git all uppity!" as verse eighteen says. He wasn't looking out for Ahasuerus; he was looking out for himself. Had Ahasuerus not been drunk he would have been able to figure that out rather quickly.

These princes, led by Memucan, told Ahasuerus that he needed to divorce his wife Vashti. Here is what he (Memucan) said:

KJV Esther 1:19 *If it please the king, let there go a royal commandment from him, and let it be written among the laws of the Persians and the Medes, that it be not altered, That Vashti come no more before king Ahasuerus; and let the king give her royal estate unto another that is better than she.* **20** *And when the king's decree which he shall make shall be published throughout all his empire, (for it is great,) all the wives shall give to their husbands honour, both to great and small.*

What he said and suggested can be summed up this way: "I've got a great idea, King. Take your beautiful, spunky wife and divorce her. Then make a law that she can never be queen again. Then tell everybody in the entire world about it. That way, even though you'll be single and have to find another wife somehow, our wives will treat us better!"

It takes a drunken fool to suggest something like that, and it takes an even bigger drunken fool to go along with it. But alas:

KJV Esther 1:21 *And the saying pleased the king and the princes; and the king did according to the word of Memucan:*

No one there had enough sense to realize how brain-dead they were all being. They were *pleased* by the idea. Tell me, men, you that believe you have a beautiful wife, how pleased would you be to no longer have your beautiful wife? Somehow, Ahasuerus was pleased by this. Five minutes earlier she was the greatest thing on Earth and so incredibly

23

hot that he was willing to violate every law and custom of Persia to show her off, and now he is instantly ready to give her up forever.

This really is a foolish king.

There Was a Flawed Message

Esther 1:22 *For he sent letters into all the king's provinces, into every province according to the writing thereof, and to every people after their language, that every man should bear rule in his own house, and that it should be published according to the language of every people.*

As you read this verse, I am pretty certain I know what you are thinking if you know your Bible. You are thinking, "That message isn't flawed, in fact, it is Biblical!" You are partially correct. Look at Ephesians 5:

Ephesians 5:22 *Wives, submit yourselves unto your own husbands, as unto the Lord.* **23** *For the husband is the head of the wife, even as Christ is the head of the church: and he is the saviour of the body.* **24** *Therefore as the church is subject unto Christ, so let the wives be to their own husbands in every thing.*

Comparing those two passages, it sounds very much like the content is basically the same in both. And if you think that you are correct, it is. Both of them basically say the same thing, that the man is to bear rule in his own home. But the message in Esther is still flawed. You see, there are two ways a message can be flawed. It can be flawed in the ***content of the message***, or it can be flawed in the ***character of the messenger.*** In Ephesians 5, we find husbands, who are supposed to bear rule in their own homes, being told to love their wives as Christ loved the church and to give themselves for their wives as Christ did for the church. But where do you find that in the message given by Ahasuerus in Esther? It isn't there. These men were intent on having the authority, but they gave no thought at all to demonstrating love and sacrifice for their wives.

If Ahasuerus would have loved his wife, this would never have even been an issue because he wouldn't have asked her to do something so wrong. It was a flawed message because he was a flawed messenger!

Men, hear me: men who love their wives like Christ loved the church just about never have to even mention the command of Ephesians 5. I have been married for eighteen years, and I have never had to remind my wife to submit to me, not once! I have made it my business to love her like crazy and to treat her like royalty and to sacrifice myself for her and to put her first, and because of that, she lets me be in charge of the home without my ever having to ask for it or demand it.

* * * * *

This book is entitled *Five Feasts and the Fingerprints Of God*, but so far all we have seen is a drunken party and a high profile divorce. But if you know anything at all about the book of Esther, you know that God was using even the sin and foolishness of Ahasuerus to accomplish His will in protecting His people. You see, our God is so much God that He can make even the sins of wicked men end up benefitting His people. So when you are going through a hard time, please,

25

remember that the God who was looking ahead in the days of Esther and making preparations for the hard days to come is also looking ahead and making preparations in your life.

Chapter 2
A Queen of Unknown Origin

Esther 2:1 *After these things, when the wrath of king Ahasuerus was appeased, he remembered Vashti, and what she had done, and what was decreed against her. 2 Then said the king's servants that ministered unto him, Let there be fair young virgins sought for the king: 3 And let the king appoint officers in all the provinces of his kingdom, that they may gather together all the fair young virgins unto Shushan the palace, to the house of the women, unto the custody of Hege the king's chamberlain, keeper of the women; and let their things for purification be given them: 4 And let the maiden which pleaseth the king be queen instead of Vashti. And the thing pleased the king; and he did so. 5 Now in Shushan the palace there was a certain Jew, whose name was Mordecai, the son of Jair, the son of Shimei, the son of Kish, a Benjamite; 6 Who had been carried away from Jerusalem with the captivity which had been carried away with Jeconiah king of Judah, whom Nebuchadnezzar the king of Babylon had carried away. 7 And he brought up Hadassah, that is, Esther, his uncle's daughter: for she had neither father nor mother, and the maid was fair and beautiful; whom Mordecai, when her father and mother were dead, took for his own daughter. 8*

So it came to pass, when the king's commandment and his decree was heard, and when many maidens were gathered together unto Shushan the palace, to the custody of Hegai, that Esther was brought also unto the king's house, to the custody of Hegai, keeper of the women. **9** *And the maiden pleased him, and she obtained kindness of him; and he speedily gave her her things for purification, with such things as belonged to her, and seven maidens, which were meet to be given her, out of the king's house: and he preferred her and her maids unto the best place of the house of the women.* **10** *Esther had not shewed her people nor her kindred: for Mordecai had charged her that she should not shew it.* **11** *And Mordecai walked every day before the court of the women's house, to know how Esther did, and what should become of her.* **12** *Now when every maid's turn was come to go in to king Ahasuerus, after that she had been twelve months, according to the manner of the women, (for so were the days of their purifications accomplished, to wit, six months with oil of myrrh, and six months with sweet odours, and with other things for the purifying of the women;)* **13** *Then thus came every maiden unto the king; whatsoever she desired was given her to go with her out of the house of the women unto the king's house.* **14** *In the evening she went, and on the morrow she returned into the second house of the women, to the custody of Shaashgaz, the king's chamberlain, which kept the concubines: she came in unto the king no more, except the king delighted in her, and that she were called by name.* **15** *Now when the turn of Esther, the daughter of Abihail the uncle of Mordecai, who had taken her for his daughter, was come to go in unto the king, she required nothing but what Hegai the* *king's chamberlain, the keeper of the women, appointed. And Esther obtained favour in the sight of all them that looked upon her.* **16** *So Esther was taken unto king Ahasuerus into his house royal in the tenth month, which is the month Tebeth, in the seventh year of his reign.* **17** *And the king loved Esther above all the women, and she obtained grace and favour in his sight more than all the virgins; so that he set the royal crown upon her head, and made her queen instead of Vashti.* **18** *Then the king made a great feast unto all his princes and his servants, even Esther's feast; and he made a release to the provinces, and gave gifts, according to the state of the king.* **19** *And when the virgins were gathered together the second time, then Mordecai sat in the king's gate.* **20** *Esther had not yet shewed her kindred nor her people; as Mordecai had charged her: for Esther did the commandment of Mordecai, like as when she was brought up with him.* **21** *In those days, while Mordecai sat in the king's gate, two of the king's chamberlains, Bigthan and Teresh, of those which kept the door, were wroth, and sought to lay hand on the king Ahasuerus.* **22** *And the thing was known to Mordecai, who told it unto Esther the queen; and Esther certified the king thereof in Mordecai's name.* **23** *And when inquisition was made of the matter, it was found out; therefore they were both hanged on a tree: and it was written in the book of the chronicles before the king.*

In chapter one of Esther we were introduced to a king that the Bible calls Ahasuerus, a man that history refers to by another of his names, Xerxes. We learned that he was a hot tempered, self-indulgent man and that he was about to go fight against Greece. In preparation for that war he held a 187 day drunken pep rally in the palace at Shushan. His wife, a spunky gal by the name of Vashti, held a feast of her own for the ladies in another area separate from the men, as the customs of the Persians dictated. But at the end of the drunken feast, King Ahasuerus asked Vashti to do something wrong, and she said no. That sent him into a drunken rage, and in his foolishness and drunkenness, he turned to his drunken counselors and asked them what they thought he should do. Their solution was that the king should divorce his beautiful wife and go through the process of finding another. As dumb as that sounds, and it is in fact actually as dumb as it sounds, he went along with it. He put his drunken hand to pen, and pen to paper, and wrote it into the law of the Medes and the Persians that Vashti could no longer be his wife or be the queen. That leads us up to the events of chapter two.

A Suggested Pageant

Esther 2:1 *After these things, when the wrath of king Ahasuerus was appeased, he remembered Vashti, and what she had done, and what was decreed against her.*

Let your attention be drawn to those first three words "After these things." I want you to focus there for a moment for a reason. Look at Esther 1:3:

Esther 1:3 *In the third year of his reign, he made a feast unto all his princes and his servants; the power of Persia and Media, the nobles and princes of the provinces, being before him:*

It was in the third year of his reign that he divorced Vashti. Now look at Esther 2:16:

Esther 2:16 *So Esther was taken unto king Ahasuerus into his house royal in the tenth month, which is the month Tebeth, in the seventh year of his reign.*

In what year of his reign did Ahasuerus marry Esther? It was the seventh year, a gap of four years time. Why does that "after these things" cover four years?

Do you remember what the 187 day party of chapter one was all about? It was a pep rally in preparation for Ahasuerus going to war against Greece. Guess how long history tells us that war and his return took? Four years. Ahasuerus got drunk, divorced his wife at his counselor's suggestion, and then had to go to war, come back, and pick a bride. He was without a queen for four years. He left for battle right after having his home split up.

Any guesses how the battle went? Not surprisingly, not so well. That Grecian campaign was an unqualified disaster for Xerxes. At Thermopylae a handful of Spartans under Leonidas checked and delayed his mighty army, and delays are very costly in battle. Later that same year Xerxes' navy of 1,400 ships was unable to overcome 380 ships of the Greeks in the Battle of Salamis. Then in 479 B.C., at Plataea, the bulk of the Persian army was destroyed. Meanwhile, the Greek fleet commanded by the king of Sparta drove the Persian fleet to the Asian mainland at Mycale. Leotychidas, the Spartan king, landed his sailors and marines farther up the coast, destroyed the Persian fleet, and inflicted heavy casualties on a supporting army. The Ionians and the Aeolians at once rose up in revolt, thus ending the Persian invasion of Greece in the final disaster for Persia.[10]

Simply put, things went very bad! Did his disaster with Vashti lead to this? Well, if you have ever been married you know that it sure didn't help matters! No man ever had troubles in his marriage without it affecting his work!

After Xerxes' return to Shushan, Herodotus tells us that he consoled himself over his shameful defeats by sensual indulgences with his harem. That dove-tails perfectly with what we read here in Esther chapter two.[11]

Esther 2:2 *Then said the king's servants that ministered unto him, Let there be fair young virgins sought for the king:* **3** *And let the king appoint officers in all the provinces of his kingdom, that they may gather together all the fair young virgins unto Shushan the palace, to the house of the women, unto the custody of Hege the king's chamberlain, keeper of the women; and let their things for purification be given them:* **4** *And let the maiden which pleaseth the king be queen instead of Vashti. And the thing pleased the king; and he did so.*

Here we have the account of what was transpiring while Ahasuerus was away. Men were dispatched from the house of the king into all of the king's provinces to look for pretty girls. Do you remember how many provinces there were and how far flung they were?

Esther 1:1 *Now it came to pass in the days of Ahasuerus, (this is Ahasuerus which reigned, from India even unto Ethiopia, over an hundred and seven and twenty provinces:)*

From the far end of India to the far end of Ethiopia is around 4,000 miles! At the time of Ahasuerus that kingdom had a population of 100 million people![12]

I point this out for two reasons, only one of which I will give you now; I will save the other one for later. The reason I will give you now for showing you this is to show you what a huge task this was and how long it would take! They needed every bit of four years to search out and select the most beautiful women from all those provinces and all those people.

Nonetheless, the idea pleased the king, so before he went into battle he commanded it to be done and so his men set about doing it.

A Star in the Palace

Esther 2:5 *Now in Shushan the palace there was a certain Jew, whose name was Mordecai, the son of Jair, the son of Shimei, the son of Kish, a Benjamite;* **6** *Who had been carried away from Jerusalem with the captivity which had been carried away with Jeconiah king of Judah, whom Nebuchadnezzar the king of Babylon had carried away.*

It is at this point in the text that we are introduced to a man named Mordecai. Not many people know his name, but he became one of the most important men who ever lived. This man was a Jew. He was from the tribe of Benjamin. His background is one that is very interesting and bears some close examination.

We are told that he was "The son of Jair, the son of Shimei, the son of Kish, a Benjamite." To our English minds, we normally think that we have just read his name along with the name of his father, his grandfather, and his great-grandfather. Let me help you understand something, though.

Who was Jesus' earthly "father?" That would be Joseph, who adopted Him. But look at this:

33

Matthew 1:1 *The book of the generation of Jesus Christ, the son of David, the son of Abraham.*

Jesus is not called the son of Joseph, He is called the son of David, a man who lived dozens of generations before Him! You say, "But he was only called that because Joseph wasn't really His father!" Wrong answer. Tell me, who was David's father? That would be Jesse. But who does Matthew 1:1 say was his father? Abraham, who lived dozens of generations before him! You see, when it came to putting information from Jewish genealogies into a narrative for people to read, they routinely skipped over names that people were not likely to know and latched on to names that everyone was likely to know. And two of the names listed in Mordecai's lineage were very familiar names to the Jews. We find the name Shimei, and we find the name Kish.

Shimei we find back in II Samuel 16. In that passage David was running for his life. His own son Absalom had led an insurrection and stolen the kingdom from him. David had to take a handful of loyal men and run into the wilderness to try to escape. And as he did so, a man named Shimei came out to meet him:

2 Samuel 16:5 *And when king David came to Bahurim, behold, thence came out a man of the family of the house of Saul, whose name was Shimei, the son of Gera: he came forth, and cursed still as he came. 6 And he cast stones at David, and at all the servants of king David: and all the people and all the mighty men were on his right hand and on his left. 7 And thus said Shimei when he cursed, Come out, come out, thou bloody man, and thou man of Belial: 8 The LORD hath returned upon thee all the blood of the house of Saul, in whose* *stead thou hast reigned; and the LORD hath delivered the kingdom into the hand of Absalom thy son: and, behold, thou art taken in thy mischief, because thou art a bloody man.* **9** *Then said Abishai the son of Zeruiah unto the king, Why should this dead dog curse my lord the king? let me go over, I pray thee, and take off his head.* **10** *And the king said, What have I to do with you, ye sons of Zeruiah? so let him curse, because the LORD hath said unto him, Curse David. Who shall then say, Wherefore hast thou done so?* **11** *And David said to Abishai, and to all his servants, Behold, my son, which came forth of my bowels, seeketh my life: how much more now may this Benjamite do it? let him alone, and let him curse; for the LORD hath bidden him.* **12** *It may be that the LORD will look on mine affliction, and that the LORD will requite me good for his cursing this day.* **13** *And as David and his men went by the way, Shimei went along on the hill's side over against him, and cursed as he went, and threw stones at him, and cast dust.*

Shimei was a dirt bag! And David, in his depression, let him live and even promised him that he would not kill him. But years later, as an old man about to die, David thought about Shimei, and he thought about his son Solomon who was about to be king, and he realized that Shimei could be a problem. Why? Because he was from the line of a man named Kish. Who was Kish?

1 Chronicles 8:33 *And Ner begat Kish, and Kish begat Saul, and Saul begat Jonathan, and Malchishua, and Abinadab, and Eshbaal.*

Kish was the father of Saul, the first king of Israel. Keep that in mind; we'll get back to it.

Realizing that Shimei could be a threat, David told Solomon to put Shimei to death. Solomon did so once Shimei showed himself to be disobedient and rebellious, unwilling to obey the commands of the king. But notice something:

1 Kings 2:8 *And, behold, thou hast with thee Shimei the son of Gera, a Benjamite of Bahurim, which cursed me with a grievous curse in the day when I went to Mahanaim: but he came down to meet me at Jordan, and I sware to him by the LORD, saying, I will not put thee to death with the sword.* **9** *Now therefore hold him not guiltless: for thou art a wise man, and knowest what thou oughtest to do unto him; but his hoar head bring thou down to the grave with blood.*

Shimei was by this time "hoary headed," meaning he was an old, white haired man.

Why am I pointing all of this out? Because it factors into what happened in the book of Esther. Do you remember that I told you the name of God is not mentioned in Esther, but His fingerprints are everywhere? An ancient Jewish writing called the Targum says, "He (Mordecai) was the son of Jair, the son of Shimei, the son of Gera, the son of Kish." And "this was the same Shimei that cursed David; and whom David forbade Joab to slay because he saw, in the spirit of prophecy, that he was to be the predecessor of Esther and Mordecai; but when he became old, and incapable of having children, David ordered Solomon to put him to death."[13]

In other words, God withheld David from killing Shimei because He needed Shimei to live long enough to produce children so that he could have a great-great-great... grandson named Mordecai, who would save all of the Jews in the entire world in the time of Esther! Friends, God knows what He is doing, and He knows what He is doing hundreds (thousands, millions) of years before He does it!

If you have ever wondered why God doesn't kill someone who, in your evaluation, desperately needs killing, maybe it's because He is going to need his or her great-great-great-great-grandchild for something important!

Esther 2:7 *And he brought up Hadassah, that is, Esther, his uncle's daughter: for she had neither father nor mother, and the maid was fair and beautiful; whom Mordecai, when her father and mother were dead, took for his own daughter.*

This man Mordecai (an old man by this time, maybe even 100 or older based on the information we find in verse six about the captivity) found himself raising his young cousin as if she were his own daughter. Her original name was Hadassah, meaning "Myrtle," like the tree. But when she came into the court of Persia she was given a Persian name, Esther, which means "A Star." That name is surely appropriate, because throughout this book she shines like a point of light in the darkest of night.

Esther 2:8 *So it came to pass, when the king's commandment and his decree was heard, and when many maidens were gathered together unto Shushan the palace, to the custody of Hegai, that Esther was brought also unto the king's house, to the custody of Hegai, keeper of the women. 9 And the maiden pleased him, and she obtained kindness of him; and he speedily gave her her things for purification, with such things as belonged to her, and seven maidens, which were meet to be given her, out of the king's house: and he* *preferred her and her maids unto the best place of the house of the women.*

The man Hegai was very important in all of this process. He was "the keeper of the women." That lets us know that he was a eunuch charged with getting these women ready for the king, observing them, and basically giving his evaluation of them. What he said and thought carried a lot of weight. Out of all of the women chosen for this pageant, somehow Hegai settled on Esther as the best and pushed her to the front of the line. She became a star in his eyes and was about to become a star in everyone else's.

A Secret of Prudence

Esther 2:10 *Esther had not shewed her people nor her kindred: for Mordecai had charged her that she should not shew it.*

This is both an instructive and a sad verse. It is sad because it shows us that anti-Semitism is not a recent thing. People have hated and despised the Jews for years. Anyone today, from Muslims, to Hollywood stars, to liberal politicians, who despise the Jews are not doing or saying anything new; they are simply following in the filthy footsteps of all of the dirty people who have come before them, from Hitler, to Stalin, to Haman, and more.

It is instructive because it teaches us something about a little-used character quality today–that thing called *prudence*. People need to grasp that just because you *could* say it doesn't mean that you *should* say it. Weigh your words carefully, and only say what actually needs to be said! Because Mordecai commanded and Esther obeyed in this matter of prudence she became queen, and her people were saved. If she had had loose lips she would not have been queen, and her people would have died.

A Setting of Prominence

Esther 2:11 *And Mordecai walked every day before the court of the women's house, to know how Esther did, and what should become of her.* **12** *Now when every maid's turn was come to go in to king Ahasuerus, after that she had been twelve months, according to the manner of the women, (for so were the days of their purifications accomplished, to wit, six months with oil of myrrh, and six months with sweet odours, and with other things for the purifying of the women;)* **13** *Then thus came every maiden unto the king; whatsoever she desired was given her to go with her out of the house of the women unto the king's house.* **14** *In the evening she went, and on the morrow she returned into the second house of the women, to the custody of Shaashgaz, the king's chamberlain, which kept the concubines: she came in unto the king no more, except the king delighted in her, and that she were called by name.*

The man Mordecai held some sort of position in the palace. He thus had access to be nearby and find out all that was happening with Esther, whom he checked on every single day.

There came a day when King Ahasuerus was back. He was in a foul mood, nursing his wounds, brooding over his losses, and plotting his revenge. But in the mean time, he needed to go ahead and select a new wife.

All of the women had undergone ceremonial purification, and they had also been oiled, perfumed, coiffed, shaped, tanned, toned, trimmed, and gussied up. Then one by one, they went for a night with the king, each one becoming either a "B-list" wife or the one and only "A-list" wife.

Many will say, "But that is debauched, wicked, godless behavior!" Yes, it was. Welcome to the wonderful world of Xerxes, Ahasuerus. It was nothing for him to have hundreds of wives and not to even bother treating them all equally. The "B-list" wives would be little more than concubines, there to serve his whims from time to time.

Verse thirteen makes a very interesting statement for us. It says:

...whatsoever she desired was given her to go with her out of the house of the women unto the king's house.

Adam Clarke said, "Whatever kind of dress stuff, colour, jewels, &c., they thought best to set off their persons, and render them more engaging, should be given them."[14] They had a blank check to get gussied up as elaborately as they liked to go see the king; they could be as extravagant as they wanted. But look at the next verse:

Esther 2:15 *Now when the turn of Esther, the daughter of Abihail the uncle of Mordecai, who had taken her for his daughter, was come to go in unto the king, she required nothing but what Hegai the king's chamberlain, the keeper of the women, appointed. And Esther obtained favour in the sight of all them that looked upon her.*

Esther did not ask for one extra thing at all. She just said to Hegai, "Whatever you think I need is fine; I'll just trust your judgment."

There is something to that, and we can learn much from it. Hegai knew the king's desires probably better than

40

anybody, otherwise he would never have held the position he held. Esther looked to the one who knew how to please the king and said, "I'll just trust your judgment." That reminds me a great deal of King Jesus and of my Bible. In my flesh, I really don't know how to please Him. But the Bible tells me exactly what He likes and doesn't like, and although sometimes I don't understand, I am willing to trust the judgment of that Book!

The text tells us that due to her sweet, trusting spirit, Esther obtained favor in the sight of *all of them that looked on her.* Do you want to know how amazing that is? It includes the women against whom she was competing for a man! Even her competition loved her. Girls, Ladies, when you have such a sweet spirit that even other single girls and ladies love you, you have achieved something great; your spirit is probably excellent!

Esther 2:16 *So Esther was taken unto king Ahasuerus into his house royal in the tenth month, which is the month Tebeth, in the seventh year of his reign.* **17** *And the king loved Esther above all the women, and she obtained grace and favour in his sight more than all the virgins; so that he set the royal crown upon her head, and made her queen instead of Vashti.*

The beauty pageant is over. Esther is the new queen, a position of incredible prominence, and the king is happy again. How happy? Look at the next verse:

Esther 2:18 *Then the king made a great feast unto all his princes and his servants, even Esther's feast; and he made a release to the provinces, and gave gifts, according to the state of the king.*

41

He made another great feast, he gave away a bunch of gifts, and he "made a release to the provinces." What is a release? He let them out of paying a bunch of their taxes. When you have gotten a politician to lower taxes, it either means they are very happy or that they are not liberals.

Esther 2:19 *And when the virgins were gathered together the second time, then Mordecai sat in the king's gate.* **20** *Esther had not yet shewed her kindred nor her people; as Mordecai had charged her: for Esther did the commandment of Mordecai, like as when she was brought up with him.*

Neither the text nor any historical records tell us exactly why there was this second gathering of all of the contestants, and it really isn't that important. What is important is that Esther, Queen Esther now, is still obeying Mordecai's command. Young people, no matter how important you get, you are never too important to obey those who raised you!

A Stunning Plot

Esther 2:21 *In those days, while Mordecai sat in the king's gate, two of the king's chamberlains, Bigthan and Teresh, of those which kept the door, were wroth, and sought to lay hand on the king Ahasuerus.* **22** *And the thing was known to Mordecai, who told it unto Esther the queen; and Esther certified the king thereof in Mordecai's name.* **23** *And when inquisition was made of the matter, it was found out; therefore they were both hanged on a tree: and it was written in the book of the chronicles before the king.*

The first twenty verses of this chapter have been all about a beauty pageant. But suddenly, at the very end of the chapter, there is a plot twist. Three verses are here to tell us of a stunning plot that took place against the life of the king. Two of his chamberlains, men who were "threshold watchers," guarders of the king's door, decided to kill him. We don't know what set them off so badly. Maybe they were angry about Vashti, or about the losses to Greece, or about the beauty pageant, or about Esther, we just don't know. But what we do know is that as guards of the king's door they were in a position to actually do the job! Very few people had enough access to assassinate the king, but these two men did.

But their plans ended up slipping out in at least one place and that was in the gate of the king. That was where the official business of the city was done. No one would be likely to suspect two of the king's chamberlains of anything nefarious while they were talking together in the gate. But there just so happened to be a man in the gate, a very careful man. A man careful enough to instruct Esther not to tell anyone what race she was. A man careful enough to listen carefully while two chamberlains seemed to be sneaking around and whispering suspiciously. Mordecai ended up finding out what these two men were up to. And to whom was Mordecai now related? That would be Esther, the new queen. So he sent her a message, she told the king, the king verified the story, and the two would-be assassins were hanged. Then a recorder wrote the entire affair down, and he wrote in down right there while the king was watching. And then the matter was forgotten.

And I bet you have forgotten something as well. At two points in this chapter, I have told you to remember something, and that we would get back to it.

I told you first of all the empire of Ahasuerus was 4,000 miles from tip to tip and had 100 million people in it. The second thing I told you was that Mordecai, and therefore Esther as well, was descended from Kish, father of Saul. That means Esther was of royal blood. Let's deal with those two things.

Ahasuerus stages a beauty pageant, and they bring in hundreds of girls from across the known world. Yet out of an empire 4,000 miles long, nearly two and a half million square miles of landmass, 100 million people, there is a girl right there in the palace under his nose, a girl that God regards as being descended from royalty, ready to be the next queen of Persia, and she is the one chosen out of all the rest! Don't you ever, ever, ever cease to be amazed at how great our God is. Even when you cannot see Him, He is in control!

Chapter 3
Murder, He Wrote

Esther 3:1 *After these things did king Ahasuerus promote Haman the son of Hammedatha the Agagite, and advanced him, and set his seat above all the princes that were with him.* **2** *And all the king's servants, that were in the king's gate, bowed, and reverenced Haman: for the king had so commanded concerning him. But Mordecai bowed not, nor did him reverence.* **3** *Then the king's servants, which were in the king's gate, said unto Mordecai, Why transgressest thou the king's commandment?* **4** *Now it came to pass, when they spake daily unto him, and he hearkened not unto them, that they told Haman, to see whether Mordecai's matters would stand: for he had told them that he was a Jew.* **5** *And when Haman saw that Mordecai bowed not, nor did him reverence, then was Haman full of wrath.* **6** *And he thought scorn to lay hands on Mordecai alone; for they had shewed him the people of Mordecai: wherefore Haman sought to destroy all the Jews that were throughout the whole kingdom of Ahasuerus, even the people of Mordecai.* **7** *In the first month, that is, the month Nisan, in the twelfth year of king Ahasuerus, they cast Pur, that is, the lot, before Haman from day to day, and from month to month, to the twelfth month, that is, the month Adar.* **8** *And*

*Haman said unto king Ahasuerus, There is a certain people scattered abroad and dispersed among the people in all the provinces of thy kingdom; and their laws are diverse from all people; neither keep they the king's laws: therefore it is not for the king's profit to suffer them. **9** If it please the king, let it be written that they may be destroyed: and I will pay ten thousand talents of silver to the hands of those that have the charge of the business, to bring it into the king's treasuries. **10** And the king took his ring from his hand, and gave it unto Haman the son of Hammedatha the Agagite, the Jews' enemy. **11** And the king said unto Haman, The silver is given to thee, the people also, to do with them as it seemeth good to thee. **12** Then were the king's scribes called on the thirteenth day of the first month, and there was written according to all that Haman had commanded unto the king's lieutenants, and to the governors that were over every province, and to the rulers of every people of every province according to the writing thereof, and to every people after their language; in the name of king Ahasuerus was it written, and sealed with the king's ring. **13** And the letters were sent by posts into all the king's provinces, to destroy, to kill, and to cause to perish, all Jews, both young and old, little children and women, in one day, even upon the thirteenth day of the twelfth month, which is the month Adar, and to take the spoil of them for a prey. **14** The copy of the writing for a commandment to be given in every province was published unto all people, that they should be ready against that day. **15** The posts went out, being hastened by the king's commandment, and the decree was given in Shushan the palace. And the king and Haman sat down to drink; but the city Shushan was perplexed.*

By the end of chapter two of the book of Esther, many really eventful things had happened. There was the 187 day drunken pep rally/party, there was the divorce of Vashti by Ahasuerus, there were a series of disastrous military losses to the Greeks, and there was the choice of Esther to be the new queen. But there was also, right at the very end of chapter two, an important little aside:

Esther 2:21 *In those days, while Mordecai sat in the king's gate, two of the king's chamberlains, Bigthan and Teresh, of those which kept the door, were wroth, and sought to lay hand on the king Ahasuerus.* **22** *And the thing was known to Mordecai, who told it unto Esther the queen; and Esther certified the king thereof in Mordecai's name.* **23** *And when inquisition was made of the matter, it was found out; therefore they were both hanged on a tree: and it was written in the book of the chronicles before the king.*

That is how chapter two ended, with Mordecai, Esther's adoptive dad, saving the king's life. But as chapter three begins, that act of valor had been forgotten. In fact, it had been forgotten so quickly that Mordecai had not even been rewarded for it in any way!

Believe me: God was behind the forgetfulness of the king. It was going to be essential for that chip to be cashed in later rather than sooner.

And that brings us to chapter three.

An Enemy Ruling

Esther 3:1 *After these things did king Ahasuerus promote Haman the son of Hammedatha the Agagite, and advanced him, and set his seat above all the princes that were* *with him.* **2a** *And all the king's servants, that were in the king's gate, bowed, and reverenced Haman...*

May I point out to you an error in the Bible? This verse really should say, "After these things did King Ahasuerus promote Mordecai." There is no error in the text, so please don't misunderstand; there will never be an error in the text. This was an error on the part of the king! Mordecai had saved his life, but it is someone else entirely that later gets promoted, for whatever reason.

The man that was promoted instead of Mordecai was a man named Haman, and his name means, are you ready for this? *Magnificent.* Now, how in the world could a person like that ever end up as a proud, pompous jerk? I just can't imagine! *Look everybody, here comes... MAGNIFICENT!*

Mr. Magnificent, Haman, had a background, one that goes way back. If you remember in the last chapter, we saw how Mordecai and Esther had a background that went way back into history, back to Shimei and Kish. Haman's background given here goes back to the exact same time period! This man is called *Haman the Agagite.* Let me remind you why that is so important:

1 Samuel 15:1 *Samuel also said unto Saul, The LORD sent me to anoint thee to be king over his people, over Israel: now therefore hearken thou unto the voice of the words of the LORD.* **2** *Thus saith the LORD of hosts, I remember that which Amalek did to Israel, how he laid wait for him in the way, when he came up from Egypt.* **3** *Now go and smite Amalek, and utterly destroy all that they have, and spare them not; but slay both man and woman, infant and suckling, ox and sheep, camel and ass.* **4** *And Saul gathered the people* together, and numbered them in Telaim, two hundred thousand footmen, and ten thousand men of Judah. **5** And Saul came to a city of Amalek, and laid wait in the valley. **6** And Saul said unto the Kenites, Go, depart, get you down from among the Amalekites, lest I destroy you with them: for ye shewed kindness to all the children of Israel, when they came up out of Egypt. So the Kenites departed from among the Amalekites. **7** And Saul smote the Amalekites from Havilah until thou comest to Shur, that is over against Egypt. **8** And he took Agag the king of the Amalekites alive, and utterly destroyed all the people with the edge of the sword. **9** But Saul and the people spared Agag, and the best of the sheep, and of the oxen, and of the fatlings, and the lambs, and all that was good, and would not utterly destroy them: but every thing that was vile and refuse, that they destroyed utterly. **10** Then came the word of the LORD unto Samuel, saying, **11** It repenteth me that I have set up Saul to be king: for he is turned back from following me, and hath not performed my commandments. And it grieved Samuel; and he cried unto the LORD all night. **12** And when Samuel rose early to meet Saul in the morning, it was told Samuel, saying, Saul came to Carmel, and, behold, he set him up a place, and is gone about, and passed on, and gone down to Gilgal. **13** And Samuel came to Saul: and Saul said unto him, Blessed be thou of the LORD: I have performed the commandment of the LORD. **14** And Samuel said, What meaneth then this bleating of the sheep in mine ears, and the lowing of the oxen which I hear? **15** And Saul said, They have brought them from the Amalekites: for the people spared the best of the sheep and of the oxen, to sacrifice unto the LORD thy God; and the rest we have utterly destroyed. **16** Then

49

Samuel said unto Saul, Stay, and I will tell thee what the LORD hath said to me this night. And he said unto him, Say on. 17 And Samuel said, When thou wast little in thine own sight, wast thou not made the head of the tribes of Israel, and the LORD anointed thee king over Israel? 18 And the LORD sent thee on a journey, and said, Go and utterly destroy the sinners the Amalekites, and fight against them until they be consumed. 19 Wherefore then didst thou not obey the voice of the LORD, but didst fly upon the spoil, and didst evil in the sight of the LORD? 20 And Saul said unto Samuel, Yea, I have obeyed the voice of the LORD, and have gone the way which the LORD sent me, and have brought Agag the king of Amalek, and have utterly destroyed the Amalekites. 21 But the people took of the spoil, sheep and oxen, the chief of the things which should have been utterly destroyed, to sacrifice unto the LORD thy God in Gilgal. 22 And Samuel said, Hath the LORD as great delight in burnt offerings and sacrifices, as in obeying the voice of the LORD? Behold, to obey is better than sacrifice, and to hearken than the fat of rams. 23 For rebellion is as the sin of witchcraft, and stubbornness is as iniquity and idolatry. Because thou hast rejected the word of the LORD, he hath also rejected thee from being king. 24 And Saul said unto Samuel, I have sinned: for I have transgressed the commandment of the LORD, and thy words: because I feared the people, and obeyed their voice. 25 Now therefore, I pray thee, pardon my sin, and turn again with me, that I may worship the LORD. 26 And Samuel said unto Saul, I will not return with thee: for thou hast rejected the word of the LORD, and the LORD hath rejected thee from being king over Israel. 27 And as Samuel turned about to go away, he laid hold upon *the skirt of his mantle, and it rent.* **28** *And Samuel said unto him, The LORD hath rent the kingdom of Israel from thee this day, and hath given it to a neighbour of thine, that is better than thou.* **29** *And also the Strength of Israel will not lie nor repent: for he is not a man, that he should repent.* **30** *Then he said, I have sinned: yet honour me now, I pray thee, before the elders of my people, and before Israel, and turn again with me, that I may worship the LORD thy God.* **31** *So Samuel turned again after Saul; and Saul worshipped the LORD.* **32** *Then said Samuel, Bring ye hither to me Agag the king of the Amalekites. And Agag came unto him delicately. And Agag said, Surely the bitterness of death is past.* **33** *And Samuel said, As thy sword hath made women childless, so shall thy mother be childless among women. And Samuel hewed Agag in pieces before the LORD in Gilgal.*

In I Samuel 15 King Saul was commanded to destroy the entire nation of Amalek, all of them. This was a nation that only cared about destroying people. They hated the Jews; they tried to destroy them. It was so bad that God told them never to forget what Amalek did:

Deuteronomy 25:17 *Remember what Amalek did unto thee by the way, when ye were come forth out of Egypt;* **18** *How he met thee by the way, and smote the hindmost of thee, even all that were feeble behind thee, when thou wast faint and weary; and he feared not God.* **19** *Therefore it shall be, when the LORD thy God hath given thee rest from all thine enemies round about, in the land which the LORD thy God giveth thee for an inheritance to possess it, that thou shalt blot out the remembrance of Amalek from under heaven; thou shalt not forget it.*

Years later, God told Saul and Israel to wipe them out, but Saul did not obey. He kept Agag alive as a trophy, a captured king to parade around. When Samuel, the priest, got there and saw the sheep still alive and Agag still alive he went ballistic. He ended up picking up a sword himself and killing Agag. That was supposed to be Saul's job.

But pay attention, please. Saul's disobedience went further than just not destroying Agag and the sheep. He also left other Amalekites alive somewhere along the line. He may have utterly destroyed all of those he came in contact with, but he obviously did not complete the job by making sure he went town to town and house to house to make sure the job was done. How do we know that? Because of Esther 3:1:

Esther 3:1 *After these things did king Ahasuerus promote Haman the son of Hammedatha **the Agagite**, and advanced him, and set his seat above all the princes that were with him.*

Haman was a descendant of that king, King Agag, that we read about in I Samuel 15! Samuel had to do the job of killing Agag, but apparently, he did not realize that Saul had also left sons or grandsons of Agag alive. How critical of a mistake was that? Well, it obviously did not seem like too big of a deal at the time but fast forward five hundred years or so to the time of Esther. Now there is an Agagite who becomes the second in command of the entire Persian Empire. Then he hatches a plot to wipe out all of the Jews in the world, and he almost succeeds. One little act of disobedience five hundred years earlier nearly cost an entire nation their lives.

There is no such thing as small disobedience to God! When you read the book of Esther, realize that none of this had to happen. If Saul had fully obeyed five hundred years earlier, there would never have even been a Haman the Agagite. The enemy of the book of Esther would never have even existed.

An Elder Refusing

Esther 3:2 *And all the king's servants, that were in the king's gate, bowed, and reverenced Haman: for the king had so commanded concerning him. But Mordecai bowed not, nor did him reverence.*

Mordecai was not being obstinate, stubborn, or rude. A look at the words used for bowed and reverenced will explain why Mordecai refused to do it.

There are different kinds of bows in Hebrew life and in the Hebrew language. The most common bow is found in the word *cara.* That is a bow of respect. That kind of bow was perfectly permissible under the Mosaic Law and in Jewish life. But that is not the kind of bow that the king commanded or that Haman expected. What he expected was *lo yichra velo yishtachaveh.* It means what the Persian kings frequently received, a species of Divine adoration, a kind of prostration which implies the highest degree of reverence that can be paid to God or man, lying down flat on the earth, with the hands and feet extended and the mouth in the dust.[15]

It was not respect that was being demanded, it was worship! It is the same type of thing that Nebuchadnezzar was asking for in Daniel chapter three. Mordecai was not going to have any part of that.

This is the second thing the king has asked for in three chapters, and this is the second time he is going to be disobeyed! First it was Vashti and now it is Mordecai. By the way, I am curious about something: why is it that the people who rip into Vashti for disobeying her husband think Mordecai was a hero for disobeying the king? Either they were both right, or they were both wrong!

Esther 3:3 *Then the king's servants, which were in the king's gate, said unto Mordecai, Why transgressest thou the king's commandment?* **4** *Now it came to pass, when they spake daily unto him, and he hearkened not unto them, that they told Haman, to see whether Mordecai's matters would stand: for he had told them that he was a Jew.*

Back in chapter two, Mordecai had commanded Esther not to tell anyone that she was a Jew. It wasn't time for that yet. But now the time to begin divulging that information has come. Mordecai told them that he was not bowing because he was a Jew. Everyone knew what that meant. It meant that the law of his God was of greater authority to him that the law of the king. Those laws were in conflict, so Mordecai chose to do right and obey God rather than man.

The servants of the king then ran to Haman and tattled on Mordecai for not bowing, and they told him why.

Mordecai was an old man, but he was an old man who wasn't about to lay down and quit on God. Thank God for senior saints who still wield the sword for the Lord!

An Evil Rising

Esther 3:5 *And when Haman saw that Mordecai bowed not, nor did him reverence, then was Haman full of wrath.* **6** *And he thought scorn to lay hands on Mordecai alone; for they had shewed him the people of Mordecai: wherefore Haman sought* *to destroy all the Jews that were throughout the whole kingdom of Ahasuerus, even the people of Mordecai.*

After the servants tattled on Mordecai, Haman started to watch for it. Sure enough, he saw Mordecai refusing to bow before him. The Bible says that he was "full of wrath at that;" he was in a homicidal rage!

But it gets worse. You see, Haman knew who he himself was and what people he was descended from. Now he also knew who Mordecai was and what people Mordecai was descended from. He knew from history that his people had tried to destroy the Jews and that the Jews had in turn tried to destroy them. It didn't work in either case. But now things were different. Now Amalek and Israel were not on even footing. Now Amalek had a descendent of Agag second in command of the most powerful nation on Earth, and the Jews were just powerless subjects without an army. This was Haman's chance to finish the job that his forefathers had started, as well as getting personal vengeance on Mordecai.

Esther 3:7 *In the first month, that is, the month Nisan, in the twelfth year of king Ahasuerus, they cast Pur, that is, the lot, before Haman from day to day, and from month to month, to the twelfth month, that is, the month Adar.*

This verse gives us some information that helps us to put the time elements together. Esther had become the queen in the seventh year of Ahasuerus' reign. It is now the twelfth year, so they have been married for four to five years. Sometime during those five years Mordecai had saved the king's life, and it had been forgotten. Now, Haman is going to try to kill Mordecai and all of his people.

The Persians were a superstitious people. One of the ways they demonstrated that superstition was by consulting methods of divination, magic, to decide when to do things. One of their favorite ways of doing that was by the use of Pur, a kind of ancient dice. They cast the dice to see what month and what day would be the best one for this genocide they had planned. It came out as the middle of the month Adar.

Do you remember me saying over and again that the fingerprints of God are everywhere in this book? What month, 1-12, does this verse tell us that they sat down and cast the dice to make this decision? The first month of the year. Guess what month Adar was? The last month of the year! In other words, God made sure that from the time the decision was made His people would have time to prepare for it so they could survive it. If it had come out as the second or third month, it would have been pretty much impossible for the Jews to mobilize in time to do anything about it.

Esther 3:8 *And Haman said unto king Ahasuerus, There is a certain people scattered abroad and dispersed among the people in all the provinces of thy kingdom; and their laws are diverse from all people; neither keep they the king's laws: therefore it is not for the king's profit to suffer them.*

By the fact that the king had promoted Haman to such a high office, it is evident that he had a great deal of confidence in him. Ahasuerus trusted Haman. Even a king is not above making a huge error in judgment in whom they choose to trust. But this error in judgment was about to turn deadly.

Haman came before King Ahasuerus and began his sales pitch. He told the king that there were certain people "scattered abroad and dispersed" all throughout his kingdom. Those words he chose and used were designed to make the Jews seem like unimportant, unstable, roaming-band-of-thieves kind of people. The truth is, the Jews were among the best subjects of the Persian Empire!

He then accused them of having laws that were "diverse from all people," and of not keeping the law of the king. The first part was true; the last part was a lie. They obeyed the law of the king completely, right up to the point where that law compelled them to disobey the law of God. These people paid their taxes and kept from stealing and did all of the good things good citizens do. But they would not worship anyone but God.

Haman then told King Ahasuerus that "it is not for the king's profit to suffer them." In other words, the king would be more benefitted by killing them than by having them live. They were "negatively affecting his bottom line."

Haman then concluded by offering a solution to this "problem."

Esther 3:9 *If it please the king, let it be written that they may be destroyed: and I will pay ten thousand talents of silver to the hands of those that have the charge of the business, to bring it into the king's treasuries.*

Do you realize what Haman has just so casually asked? "King, let's just destroy an entire race of people, okey dokey?"

Of course, that kind of business takes money. And not only would it take money to do the job, it would also result in the loss of a great deal of tax revenue for the king. These people who were supposedly so wicked and awful were actually tax paying members of society. In one verse he has told the king it is "not for his profit" to let them live and in the very next verse he is acknowledging that it is going to cost the king a ton to get rid of them. So in order to overcome those possible obstacles in the mind of Ahasuerus, Haman offered to cover all of the expenses and losses. He did so to the tune of ten thousand talents of silver.

That is not a familiar monetary amount to us, so let's convert it into modern money, shall we? A talent of silver equaled about 100 pounds. There are 12 troy ounces per pound, troy being the scale used to measure precious metals. So there are 1200 ounces per talent of silver. 1200 ounces times 10,000 talents equals 12,000,000 ounces. On ounce of silver as of today (May 5, 2012) goes for $30.38. Let's just round it off to $30.00. 12,000,000 times $30 equals $360,000,000! This guy Haman was loaded, which may explain why the king installed him as his right hand man.

Most rich people love their money way too much to part with it. But for Haman, hate was more powerful than love, meaning that he hated the Jews more than he loved his money.

Esther 3:10 *And the king took his ring from his hand, and gave it unto Haman the son of Hammedatha the Agagite, the Jews' enemy.*

The king's ring was a signet with his official seal on it. Whenever a document had a blob of wax dropped onto it and the king's signet pressed into it, it became the absolute law of the land. Even the king himself could no longer change it. We saw that in Daniel chapter six where something like that caused Daniel to go into the den of lions. When Ahasuerus gave Haman his signet ring he was telling him, "Write whatever you want into law, you don't even have to consult me about the wording, just handle it, and whatever you say goes."

Ahasuerus was giving his name to Haman! It would be the same as you giving someone complete power of attorney over all of your affairs. Most parents will not even give their own children that kind of power, but Ahasuerus gave a wicked man, to whom he was not even related, that kind of awesome authority.

Esther 3:11 *And the king said unto Haman, The silver is given to thee, the people also, to do with them as it seemeth good to thee.*

Haman was either one of the luckiest men alive or one of the shrewdest men alive, at least up to this point. I do not know if he calculated that this would happen or if he just lucked into it, but one way or the other, this was working out really well for him. He offered to pay the king's treasuries $360,000,000 to destroy the Jews, and the king basically said, "No, don't worry about that, I'll foot the bill for everything. You can have the money to do the job, you can have the lives of all those you seek, and you don't have to pay me anything."

Haman had to feel like he had just won the lottery!

Esther 3:12 *Then were the king's scribes called on the thirteenth day of the first month, and there was written according to all that Haman had commanded unto the king's lieutenants, and to the governors that were over every province, and to the rulers of every people of every province according to the writing thereof, and to every people after their language; in the name of king Ahasuerus was it written,* *and sealed with the king's ring. 13 And the letters were sent by posts into all the king's provinces, to destroy, to kill, and to cause to perish, all Jews, both young and old, little children and women, in one day, even upon the thirteenth day of the twelfth month, which is the month Adar, and to take the spoil of them for a prey. 14 The copy of the writing for a commandment to be given in every province was published unto all people, that they should be ready against that day.*

Haman had the ring and now the command went out for all of the royal scribes to assemble. He dictated to them his murderous plans, and there was a copy of it translated into every language of the empire. Then one by one Haman walked down the line, someone dropped a blob of wax onto each document, he balled up his angry fist, and pressed that ring into it.

I can imagine the devil howling with delight at each and every stop along the way. Demons had to be hissing in approval. The Jews were about to be destroyed from off the face of the Earth.

But what could Haman write that could accomplish such a huge and evil task? He knew just the thing. He wrote in verse thirteen that whoever killed them could take their possessions for themselves. Greed was going to become the carrot by which he convinced the entire empire to take a stick to the Jews.

Esther 3:15 *The posts went out, being hastened by the king's commandment, and the decree was given in Shushan the palace. And the king and Haman sat down to drink; but the city Shushan was perplexed.*

Once all of the documents were sealed with the king's signet, the messengers left with blazing speed having to get these documents into every corner of the empire in time to do the job. You know that everyone had to wonder what in the world was going on. There had never been such a flurry of activity like this before.

And then a herald stepped up to his place right in Shushan the palace, and he spoke loudly and clearly:

It is decreed by Ahasuerus, great King of Persia, that on the thirteenth day of the month Adar of this very year, that all of the Jews, man, woman, child, and infant, in every province of Persia shall be destroyed, killed, murdered, by whatever means necessary, by everyone who comes in contact with them. All of the possessions of the Jews shall become the sole property of the person who kills them. This order is now the law of the Persians which alters not. Let this order be carried out in full, in the name of the great King Ahasuerus, may he live forever.

The Bible tells us that after that decree was made in the palace, two things happened. Number one, the king and Haman sat down to drink. For a man who had already lost plenty to his penchant for booze, it seems like he would have learned by now to stay away from the bottle. But here he is again, having signed the death warrant for millions of people, he and Haman sit down to throw back a brew or two, like he has just signed an order for garbage pickup to be on Tuesday instead of on Monday. This is just no big deal to him at all.

But the second thing that happened is that "the city Shushan was perplexed." It means what you think it means. People were thinking, "Did I hear that right? No, I must have misunderstood, that can't be right. The Jews are good and loyal subjects; they haven't caused a bit of trouble. There must be some misunderstanding. Why would the king kill so many good citizens? We must have missed something!"

But they hadn't. It was all true, every bit of it.

What are we to learn from all of this? Two things primarily. Number one, never underestimate the devil's hatred of the Jews. When you hear people in our day denying the Holocaust under Hitler, please, remember how ridiculous they are to doubt it, because it wasn't even the first time it had been tried!

But number two, we need to learn how dangerous it is to let wicked people make our decisions for us. We let the Word of God make our decisions, not Sodomites in San Francisco, not some atheistic teacher, not some liberal news anchor, not a socialist newspaper editor. The day we take off our signet ring and hand it to someone who doesn't believe the Bible and let them make our decisions for us is the day that we are putting ourselves and everyone that matters to us at incalculable risk.

Chapter 4

A Reluctant Heroine

Esther 4:1 *When Mordecai perceived all that was done, Mordecai rent his clothes, and put on sackcloth with ashes, and went out into the midst of the city, and cried with a loud and a bitter cry; 2 And came even before the king's gate: for none might enter into the king's gate clothed with sackcloth. 3 And in every province, whithersoever the king's commandment and his decree came, there was great mourning among the Jews, and fasting, and weeping, and wailing; and many lay in sackcloth and ashes. 4 So Esther's maids and her chamberlains came and told it her. Then was the queen exceedingly grieved; and she sent raiment to clothe Mordecai, and to take away his sackcloth from him: but he received it not. 5 Then called Esther for Hatach, one of the king's chamberlains, whom he had appointed to attend upon her, and gave him a commandment to Mordecai, to know what it was, and why it was. 6 So Hatach went forth to Mordecai unto the street of the city, which was before the king's gate. 7 And Mordecai told him of all that had happened unto him, and of the sum of the money that Haman had promised to pay to the king's treasuries for the Jews, to destroy them. 8 Also he gave him the copy of the writing of the decree that was given at*

Shushan to destroy them, to shew it unto Esther, and to declare it unto her, and to charge her that she should go in unto the king, to make supplication unto him, and to make request before him for her people. 9 And Hatach came and told Esther the words of Mordecai. 10 Again Esther spake unto Hatach, and gave him commandment unto Mordecai; 11 All the king's servants, and the people of the king's provinces, do know, that whosoever, whether man or woman, shall come unto the king into the inner court, who is not called, there is one law of his to put him to death, except such to whom the king shall hold out the golden sceptre, that he may live: but I have not been called to come in unto the king these thirty days. 12 And they told to Mordecai Esther's words. 13 Then Mordecai commanded to answer Esther, Think not with thyself that thou shalt escape in the king's house, more than all the Jews. 14 For if thou altogether holdest thy peace at this time, then shall there enlargement and deliverance arise to the Jews from another place; but thou and thy father's house shall be destroyed: and who knoweth whether thou art come to the kingdom for such a time as this? 15 Then Esther bade them return Mordecai this answer, 16 Go, gather together all the Jews that are present in Shushan, and fast ye for me, and neither eat nor drink three days, night or day: I also and my maidens will fast likewise; and so will I go in unto the king, which is not according to the law: and if I perish, I perish. 17 So Mordecai went his way, and did according to all that Esther had commanded him.

As Esther chapter three closed out, the decree that the Jews were to be destroyed had been sent out across the Persian Empire. The people there in the palace at Shushan were perplexed; they did not understand why the king would allow so many of his loyal subjects to be murdered. But in the king's chambers, King Ahasuerus and his right-hand man, Haman (the would-be destroyer), sat down to drink! They popped the top on a couple of brews, kicked back in their lazy-boys, fired up the big-screen tv, and watched the big game like nothing major had happened.

The king was pretty much oblivious. But not Haman. Haman was putting on the performance of a lifetime. He had sold the king on this plan of destruction by telling him that these people would cause harm to the king. But he knew the real reason he was doing it even if the king didn't. Haman was taking out vengeance on Mordecai over a personal grudge. Mordecai had refused to bow and worship him, and Haman was going to destroy an entire race of people because of it. But he wasn't going to tell the king that; that would not look so good to the king. So he sat back, drank, smiled, and never let on to the raging hatred in his heart towards the people he had just convinced the king to annihilate.

Haman fooled the king. Haman was ahead of the king. Haman was manipulating the king. But there was another, a person in higher authority than the king, one that Haman had not considered and, in fact, did not even believe in. The very God of Abraham, Isaac, and Jacob, the God who said in **Genesis 12:3** *I will bless them that bless thee and curse them that curse thee* had not been fooled, was not behind, and was immune to Haman's manipulation. That God had already taken steps to get ahead of Haman and that truth would begin to be made manifest in the events of Esther chapter four.

A Heartbreak

Esther 4:1 *When Mordecai perceived all that was done, Mordecai rent his clothes, and put on sackcloth with ashes, and went out into the midst of the city, and cried with a loud and a bitter cry; **2** And came even before the king's gate: for none might enter into the king's gate clothed with sackcloth. **3** And in every province, whithersoever the king's commandment and his decree came, there was great mourning among the Jews, and fasting, and weeping, and wailing; and many lay in sackcloth and ashes.*

Throughout the Bible people demonstrated sorrow by the usage of sackcloth.

Genesis 37:34 *And Jacob rent his clothes, and put sackcloth upon his loins, and mourned for his son many days.*

2 Samuel 3:31 *And David said to Joab, and to all the people that were with him, Rend your clothes, and gird you with sackcloth, and mourn before Abner. And king David himself followed the bier.*

Amos 8:10 *And I will turn your feasts into mourning, and all your songs into lamentation; and I will bring up sackcloth upon all loins, and baldness upon every head; and I will make it as the mourning of an only son, and the end thereof as a bitter day.*

Sackcloth was exactly what its name seems to imply. It was the course, rough fabric used to make sacks for carrying produce and other supplies. It was never intended to be worn. If you were to go down to an old-fashioned feed and seed and find an old rough burlap sack with seed or potatoes in it, you would have a good idea of the concept of sackcloth. It would just about peel your skin off it was so rough. For people to wear it as clothing showed extreme anguish and sorrow.

At other times people would pour ashes upon themselves as a sign of great sorrow.

2 Samuel 13:19 *And Tamar put ashes on her head, and rent her garment of divers colours that was on her, and laid her hand on her head, and went on crying.*

Job 42:6 *Wherefore I abhor myself, and repent in dust and ashes.*

Jeremiah 25:34 *Howl, ye shepherds, and cry; and wallow yourselves in the ashes, ye principal of the flock: for the days of your slaughter and of your dispersions are accomplished; and ye shall fall like a pleasant vessel.*

Ashes were most commonly put on the head as a sign that one had lost a husband, wife, or someone else important to them. Putting ashes on your head let everyone know that things were very bad for you for one reason or another. To use either sackcloth or ashes was a sign of anguish and distress.

But eight times in the Bible, an unusual thing happened. Eight times sackcloth and ashes are mentioned together. And in one particular chapter of the Bible, only one, sackcloth and ashes are mentioned twice. That chapter of the Bible is the very one we are now studying. In verse one and verse three we see the use of sackcloth and ashes together. That tells us that Esther chapter four marks one of the darkest, most anguish-filled days this world has ever seen. There really would not be another day quite like this until somewhere around the late 1930s, when a man named Hitler hatched the same type of a plan that Haman had devised nearly 3,000 years earlier. When the Bible tells us that Mordecai was in sackcloth and ashes, it lets us know that he knew just how very bad it was. When verse three tells us that in every single province of Persia, across the entire world, that many Jews did the exact same thing that Mordecai was doing, it lets us know that they all knew how bad it was as well.

These people had never heard of Mordecai! There was no social media available to them. No one "tweeted" to 10 million followers for everyone to dress the same way at the exact same time as a sign of solidarity. No, this world-wide usage of sackcloth and ashes was just the natural response to a coming world-wide holocaust of the Jews.

For just a moment before we move forward we should look at something that is noted in verse two.

Esther 4:2 *And came even before the king's gate: for none might enter into the king's gate clothed with sackcloth.*

Mordecai, once he was clothed in those signs of mourning, was able to come up to the king's gate, but he was no longer allowed to actually enter into it. Remember that in Bible times the gate of the city was where official business was conducted. It was a chamber, usually two stories high, with rooms on the sides. Previously, Mordecai had been quite welcome in the king's gate:

Esther 2:21 *In those days, while Mordecai sat **in the king's gate**, two of the king's chamberlains, Bigthan and Teresh, of those which kept the door, were wroth, and sought to lay hand on the king Ahasuerus.*

Yet in chapter four he was no longer welcome. What had changed? Was he not still the same man? Yes, he was. This was still Mordecai; this was still the same man who saved the king's life by telling what he overheard while in the king's gate. But now he was no longer welcome in the king's gate because he was wearing sackcloth.

What was that all about? The law forbade anyone from coming into the king's gate while wearing the garments of mourning. In other words, everything around the king had to be a "happy place!" It didn't matter to him whether or not things were actually *going wrong* out there with his people; it only mattered to him that he not be *bothered* by anything going wrong with his people!

That is a pathetic excuse for a leader of any kind. This man should have cared when his people were hurting, but all he cared for was himself. No leader–parent/pastor/President/ PTA captain–should take that approach. If you don't care, you shouldn't be leading! If people's problems are a bother to you, you need to get some things set right in your heart.

Esther 4:4 *So Esther's maids and her chamberlains came and told it her. Then was the queen exceedingly grieved; and she sent raiment to clothe Mordecai, and to take away his sackcloth from him: but he received it not.*

In this one verse we see the entire philosophy of modern political leadership summed up. Mordecai was out front of the gate, clothed in sackcloth and ashes. Someone came and told Queen Esther about it. By her response, what is it very clear that she thought the problem was? *The clothes of mourning!* She had it in her mind that the problem could be fixed by sending out comfortable clothes to Mordecai so he could get rid of those mourning garments.

But the garments weren't the problem. When someone was wearing sackcloth and ashes, they were doing so for a reason. The sackcloth and ashes were just a symbol of some

69

great anguish and heartbreak. Getting rid of the clothes and getting into something more comfortable was not going to work as a solution because the clothes weren't the problem!

This practice of using surface solutions to heart-deep problems is everywhere, especially in our day. A child misbehaves, so instead of teaching him right and wrong we automatically look for a medication to keep him half-doped up till we get him grown up and out of the house. Teenagers start sleeping around, so we get them condoms and shots and counseling on how to avoid unwanted pregnancies instead of reminding them that God expects them to stay virgins till they get married. A married couple starts having some issues in intimacy, so they bring pornography into the home instead of getting godly counseling or medical help to fix the actual problem. A kid goes off to college, signs up to major in Sociology or Old English Literature, and then when they graduate and can't get a job because Sociologists and Old English Lit majors don't actually produce anything, we give them a government check instead of telling them that they should have taken something useful like computer programming or welding or plumbing or architectural design. A kid throws temper tantrums until he gets what he wants, and instead of paddling the child we sign him up for the "Total Fix Your Child with Words Alone Program."

People apply surface solutions to heart-deep problems, and all that ever does is cover up something that needs to be fixed instead.

Mordecai knew this. That is why he refused the nice clothes. He sent them right back to her with a, "Thanks, but no thanks."

Esther 4:5 *Then called Esther for Hatach, one of the king's chamberlains, whom he had appointed to attend upon her, and gave him a commandment to Mordecai, to know what it was, and why it was.* **6** *So Hatach went forth to Mordecai unto the street of the city, which was before the king's gate.* **7** *And Mordecai told him of all that had happened unto him, and of the sum of the money that Haman had promised to pay to the king's treasuries for the Jews, to destroy them.* **8** *Also he gave him the copy of the writing of the decree that was given at Shushan to destroy them, to shew it unto Esther, and to declare it unto her, and to charge her that she should go in unto the king, to make supplication unto him, and to make request before him for her people.* **9** *And Hatach came and told Esther the words of Mordecai.*

When the messengers got back to Esther carrying the clothes she had sent to Mordecai, clothes that he refused, she seems to have gotten the idea that there was something very deeply wrong. So she sent a chamberlain to Mordecai and had him ask him what was wrong. This is what she should have done the first time.

Mordecai told Hatach, the chamberlain, everything that had happened in detail. But he didn't just say it; he proved it. Yes, Esther was family, but an accusation as big as the one he was about to make was too huge for anyone to just claim to be true. Mordecai pulled the decree off of the post, handed it to Hatach, and said, "Show this to Esther; here is the proof of what I am saying." This is a good pattern to follow! People who make accusations with no proof or no name are cowards. Mordecai knew better. He gave his name, and he sent the proof to Queen Esther.

A Heroine

Esther 4:10 *Again Esther spake unto Hatach, and gave him commandment unto Mordecai; **11** All the king's servants, and the people of the king's provinces, do know, that whosoever, whether man or woman, shall come unto the king into the inner court, who is not called, there is one law of his to put him to death, except such to whom the king shall hold out the golden sceptre, that he may live: but I have not been called to come in unto the king these thirty days. **12** And they told to Mordecai Esther's words.*

Once upon a time, many years prior to the events of Esther chapter four, there was a Median king named Deioces. He enacted the law that no one could come into the king's inner chamber without being called for. If they did and the king did not hold out the golden scepter to them, they would be killed. When the Persian Empire absorbed all of the territories once jointly held by Media/Persia, this law remained in place.[16]

Now, all of these years later, Esther is being told by Mordecai, "You need to go talk to the king because all of the Jews are about to be slaughtered!"

But Esther sent word back saying, "I can't! There's this law that forbids me from going to see him unless he calls for me. He hasn't called for me for thirty days! If I go before him, since he is the king, I will be disobeying both my husband and the law."

Well, now, that just settles it, doesn't it! I mean after all, a woman always has to obey her husband no matter what, right? So I guess we have to conclude that Esther did wrong.

She should have obeyed her husband and obeyed the law and not come in since her husband had *not* called for her.

Do you see the irony? Let me be a little more plain: When we speak of Queen Vashti, who disobeyed her husband by *not coming when he called her,* there will always be someone who pops up and says, "She was wrong! A woman is never to disobey her husband!" But when we speak of Queen Esther, who disobeyed that exact same husband by *coming when he had not called her,* all of the sudden she is a heroine! You can't have it both ways. Either both of them were right or both of them were wrong.

The truth is, when the law of a husband contradicts the law of God, the law of God must be followed, not the law of the husband.

Acts 5:29 *Then Peter and the other apostles answered and said, We ought to obey God rather than men.*

Esther was afraid of going against her husband–afraid that she may end up being killed. A woman ought to never be looking for a reason to go against her husband, but no woman ought to ever be afraid of her husband either!

Esther sent word to Mordecai, "I can't go in. I haven't been called for in thirty days for some reason. It seems like I've fallen out of favor with him, and if I go in, I could be killed."

Here was Mordecai's response to her:

Esther 4:13 *Then Mordecai commanded to answer Esther, Think not with thyself that thou shalt escape in the king's house, more than all the Jews.* **14** *For if thou altogether holdest thy peace at this time, then shall there enlargement and deliverance arise to the Jews from another place; but thou* *and thy father's house shall be destroyed: and who knoweth whether thou art come to the kingdom for such a time as this?*

Esther was concerned for her own safety. It seems as though she had gotten very comfortable in the king's house. Mordecai sent her word and reminded her to check that decree very carefully. Do you remember what it said?

Esther 3:13 *And the letters were sent by posts into all the king's provinces, to destroy, to kill, and to cause to perish, **all Jews**, both young and old, little children **and women**, in one day, even upon the thirteenth day of the twelfth month, which is the month Adar, and to take the spoil of them for a prey.*

That decree was written in the law of the Persians which always had to be followed to the exact letter of the law. "All" included Esther. "Women" were mentioned right there along with men. Just like Darius in Daniel chapter six found out, the king himself could not change or stop one bit of any Persian law. Maybe Ahasuerus would want to protect Esther once the slaughter started. It wouldn't matter. He couldn't. He wouldn't be allowed to. Esther was just as much at risk in the palace as a poverty stricken Jew living under a bridge somewhere.

Mordecai did have faith concerning all of this. He told Esther that, one way or another, the Jews would be saved. It seems that he remembered the promise that God made to Abraham, Isaac, and Jacob. Whether Esther saved them or not, God had already promised to preserve them; they would not be completely destroyed. But how many would die in the mean time? How few of them would be left to rebuild a people? And furthermore, he told her that if she didn't do right she and her family would be destroyed.

Have you ever considered that? Was Mordecai just guessing at that? Was he just "assuming" that God would be displeased if Esther did not help and would thus allow Esther and her family to be killed while others would be saved? What do you think?

The answer is no. Mordecai was not just guessing; he was not assuming anything. He knew that what he was saying was true. How? Why? Because Haman was destroying an entire race of people not because of that entire race but because of one man in that race. Yes, certainly, he hated the Jews in general because of the ancient grievances between the Jews and the Agagites, but he hated Mordecai specifically. It was Mordecai that had refused to bow before him. When the slaughter started, there was one family above all else that Haman was going to make sure ended up dead—the family of Mordecai. Haman did not yet know that Esther and Mordecai were related. He did not even know yet that Esther was Jew! But believe me, when he found out, on the day of the slaughter, he absolutely would have made sure that she ended up dead as well. Of course, he would have blamed it on that pesky and inflexible "law of the Persians" thing to try and save his own life with the king, but Mordecai and Esther and all of their family would absolutely end up dead, and Mordecai knew it.

I love what Mordecai said to Esther at the end of verse fourteen. It is one of the most classic and oft-quoted portions of Scripture.

Esther 4:14 *For if thou altogether holdest thy peace at this time, then shall there enlargement and deliverance arise to the Jews from another place; but thou and thy father's house shall be destroyed:* ***and who knoweth whether thou art come to the kingdom*** ***for such a time as this?***

In effect, Mordecai said, "Esther, do you think it is an accident that you ended up so beautiful? Do you think it is coincidence that you ended up growing up right here in the palace where you could be noticed? Do you think it is just happenstance that you ended up being chosen as queen instead of all the hundreds of other pretty girls? Esther, you know better. There is no 'luck' with God, there is only providence. God put you here, **in** this time, **in** this place, **for** this reason."

May I say that God has you in this time, in your place, for a reason? The best thing in the world you can do is find that reason and do it! If you do not find and do the will of God for your life, no matter how successful you become, you have wasted your life.

Esther had received her answer back from Mordecai. Now she had a choice to make. And she did.

Esther 4:16b *...and so will I go in unto the king, which is not according to the law: and if I perish, I perish.*

Did she want to go? No! Who would? She is about to take possibly her last few breaths on Earth. She is walking into the presence of a moody monarch with a habit of killing people for no really good reason. She finally had to just come to the place where she said, "I'm going in, I am going to do God's will for my life, and if I die, I die."

That is the attitude every last one of us ought to have! We ought to be determined to do God's will for our life, even if we end up getting killed for doing it. Mocking shouldn't stop us, teasing shouldn't stop us, shunning shouldn't stop us, deprivation shouldn't stop us, heartbreak shouldn't stop us, threat of death shouldn't stop us; we have been called to this task at this time at this place for such a time as this!

Some Helpers

Esther 4:15 *Then Esther bade them return Mordecai this answer,* **16** *Go, gather together all the Jews that are present in Shushan, and fast ye for me, and neither eat nor drink three days, night or day: I also and my maidens will fast likewise; and so will I go in unto the king, which is not according to the law: and if I perish, I perish.* **17** *So Mordecai went his way, and did according to all that Esther had commanded him.*

Esther was about to face the most difficult task of her life and maybe the last task of her life. But she had enough sense not to do so alone. She had been asked to do something incredibly difficult, so it was only fair that she be allowed to expect some help! She asked Mordecai and all the Jews to go before God in fasting for three days. She got all of her maidens to go before God in fasting for three days.

There are two main things that we should really notice from this. One, that we better not be in too big of a hurry to get God involved. If the entire fate of our nation were hanging in the balance, when would we go in and see the king? That very day, that very minute most likely! But Esther took three days time to prepare for it by getting with God. We very much underestimate just how important this is. It is essential that we spend personal, serious time with God, especially when facing major trials.

The second thing to notice is that the people that were needing her help were willing to help her. Do you know what most people have learned to do these days? Most people have learned to sit around and expect everyone to help them, without them ever trying to help those that are helping them! These Jews understood that the task was too great for Esther alone. She would be the tip of the spear, she would be the face of the movement, but she needed help.

Kids, you better help your parents as they help you. Clean your room, do the dishes, mow the lawn, take out the trash, do your homework, go to bed on time, get up on time.

Members, you better help your pastor as he helps you. Pray for him, provide for him, treat him and his family well, and make sure they have a good roof over their heads and good vehicles to drive.

Americans, you better help your soldiers as they help you. Pray for their protection, speak up for them, buy their coffee and their meals when you meet them in public.

Citizens, you better help your police officers as they help you. Don't pitch a fit when you get a ticket, pull over in safe locations, never allow anyone to speak ill of them.

Don't you ever be guilty of expecting others to work like a dog for you without you working like a dog for them! Don't you ever be guilty of expecting others to risk things for you without being willing to risk things for them! Don't you ever be guilty of expecting others to have your back if you are unwilling to have theirs. Don't you ever be guilty of receiving and receiving and receiving without giving and giving and giving. If there is something that someone needs to do, then there will almost always be a need for people to help as well!

Esther was scared, yes. Esther was the person most immediately in danger, yes. She was a reluctant heroine, yes. But she was also a woman willing to overcome her reluctance and just do what needed to be done.

Chapter 5

Putting a Worm on the Hook

Esther 5:1 *Now it came to pass on the third day, that Esther put on her royal apparel, and stood in the inner court of the king's house, over against the king's house: and the king sat upon his royal throne in the royal house, over against the gate of the house.* **2** *And it was so, when the king saw Esther the queen standing in the court, that she obtained favour in his sight: and the king held out to Esther the golden sceptre that was in his hand. So Esther drew near, and touched the top of the sceptre.* **3** *Then said the king unto her, What wilt thou, queen Esther? and what is thy request? it shall be even given thee to the half of the kingdom.* **4** *And Esther answered, If it seem good unto the king, let the king and Haman come this day unto the banquet that I have prepared for him.* **5** *Then the king said, Cause Haman to make haste, that he may do as Esther hath said. So the king and Haman came to the banquet that Esther had prepared.* **6** *And the king said unto Esther at the banquet of wine, What is thy petition? and it shall be granted thee: and what is thy request? even to the half of the kingdom it shall be performed.* **7** *Then answered Esther, and said, My petition and my request is;* **8** *If I have found favour in the sight of the king, and if it please the king to grant my* *petition, and to perform my request, let the king and Haman come to the banquet that I shall prepare for them, and I will do to morrow as the king hath said.* **9** *Then went Haman forth that day joyful and with a glad heart: but when Haman saw Mordecai in the king's gate, that he stood not up, nor moved for him, he was full of indignation against Mordecai.* **10** *Nevertheless Haman refrained himself: and when he came home, he sent and called for his friends, and Zeresh his wife.* **11** *And Haman told them of the glory of his riches, and the multitude of his children, and all the things wherein the king had promoted him, and how he had advanced him above the princes and servants of the king.* **12** *Haman said moreover, Yea, Esther the queen did let no man come in with the king unto the banquet that she had prepared but myself; and to morrow am I invited unto her also with the king.* **13** *Yet all this availeth me nothing, so long as I see Mordecai the Jew sitting at the king's gate.* **14** *Then said Zeresh his wife and all his friends unto him, Let a gallows be made of fifty cubits high, and to morrow speak thou unto the king that Mordecai may be hanged thereon: then go thou in merrily with the king unto the banquet. And the thing pleased Haman; and he caused the gallows to be made.*

In the waning days of World War II the Brits and their allies pulled off one of the greatest ruses and traps in history. It was evident to everyone that their next logical move was the invasion of Italy through Sicily. As such, German forces were dug in deep, waiting for the invasion to come. Something needed to be done to draw their attention away and make them think the invasion would come elsewhere. The something that they settled upon was "Operation Mincemeat." They rounded up the body of a recently deceased citizen. They created an identity and a life history for him. They dressed him as a member of the British Air Force and strapped a briefcase to his arm. That briefcase contained plans for the allied invasion to come hundreds of miles away. They set the body adrift where it would wash up onto the coast of Spain where they knew the Germans would end up in possession of it. Sure enough, they did. They checked the man's identity and history exceptionally well, and everything checked out. They bought the ruse; they took the bait—hook, line, and sinker. When the real invasion came, the Allies met almost no resistance. This was one of the greatest traps in history.[17]

But the all time greatest trap just might be what we find in Esther chapter five. If you remember from chapter four, Esther was in a bind. All of the Jews were going to be destroyed. She was in a position to try and help: she was the queen, the wife of King Ahasuerus. But the law of the Persians forbade anyone from coming into the court to see the king unless he or she had specifically been called for. If someone came to see the king without being called for, they would be killed unless, that is, the king chose to hold out the golden scepter to them and let them touch it. That would be his way of saying, "You have found grace in my sight; I will let you live."

Ahasuerus was not the kind of king in whose eyes people tended to find grace. He was more of a "kill them all and ask questions later" kind of a king. Furthermore, Esther seems to have somehow fallen out of favor with him at that time. He had not called for her in thirty days! Going in to him to ask for help was likely to result in her death.

She came to the right conclusion. That conclusion was *I'm going to do what's right, and if I die, I die.* She and her maidens fasted for three days; Mordecai and the Jews in the palace fasted for three days. There was a three day gap of time between chapter four and five where these people got hold of God and begged for His help.

And that brings us up to Esther chapter five and the trap set for wicked Haman.

The Wisdom of Esther

Esther 5:1 *Now it came to pass on the third day, that Esther put on her royal apparel, and stood in the inner court of the king's house, over against the king's house: and the king sat upon his royal throne in the royal house, over against the gate of the house.*

Let me give you a brief description of the normal surroundings of the Persian king, as described by archaeological evidence. The Persian kings normally spent their day in a two-chambered type of palace, called the inner court. People would enter into the first chamber, which was open and visible to the king on his throne. It would be like the vestibule of the church if we took out the wall separating the auditorium and the vestibule. The king would be on the platform on an elevated golden throne. People would have to walk into and through the first chamber to get to the large chamber where the king and the throne were.

In that first chamber would be guards. They had exactly one purpose: keep people from the king. Anyone trying to get into the second chamber where the king was would have to come through the first chamber, and those guards were not going to let that happen. Whoever came in would be stopped.

The guards who stopped the person entering would then turn and look at the king. The king would take a look at whom they had detained and then he would either do something... or nothing. If he did nothing, if he just sat there and did not say a word, the person who had entered would be dragged out and executed immediately.

But if he did something, a very specific something, if he held out a golden scepter that all Persian kings carried, it was a sign that the uninvited visitor was to be allowed to live and to pass by the guards and come directly before the king. In this case, he did just that!

Is that not a nearly flawless picture of our access to the King of kings? As Hebrews 4:16 says, we are able to come boldly before the throne of grace! We know that the Father will extend the scepter of grace to us every single time and that we will never be turned away. We have been given access by the blood of Christ, and every time Law and Justice turn to look at the Father, He says, "Step aside, let that one come immediately before Me!"

Esther had fasted for three days. She then cleaned up, put on the nicest garments of the queen, her "royal apparel," and walked into that first chamber. Her heart had to be beating a mile a minute, wondering if she would live or die.

Esther 5:2 *And it was so, when the king saw Esther the queen standing in the court, that she obtained favour in his sight: and the king held out to Esther the golden sceptre that was in his hand. So Esther drew near, and touched the top of the sceptre.*

It is interesting to think of the change in Ahasuerus. In chapter one he had a wife put away because she would not come when he called for her. Now in chapter four he extends grace to a wife when she comes without being called for. It seems that maybe he had at least learned a little bit from his earlier foolishness! He extended the scepter, and Esther gladly came forward and touched it.

Esther 5:3 *Then said the king unto her, What wilt thou, queen Esther? and what is thy request? it shall be even given thee to the half of the kingdom.*

Four times in the Bible a king is mentioned as offering to give someone up to half of his kingdom. Three of those times are in the book of Esther! Ahasuerus thought a great deal of this woman.

Ancient kings often made this promise; it was sort of a tradition. But I am not aware of a single example from history where anyone actually attempted to take a king up on that offer. Can anyone guess why? There is a word for a person that has half of a king's kingdom: that word is "enemy." Anyone possessing the other half of the kingdom would immediately become a threat to be dealt with!

The promise to give up to half of the kingdom was never a promise that anyone would try to get a king to literally fulfill. It was a promise that the king was willing to give abundantly to whomever the person was; the king was willing to be lavish and generous with them. This was sort of like a blank check for Esther. If she had asked for ten thousand talents of silver, he would have given it to her. If she had asked for apes and camels and slaves to be given to her, he would have done it. If she had asked for an entire wardrobe of new clothes and shoes, he would have said yes.

But Esther had something far greater in mind. She also had a lot of wisdom in how she went about getting it.

Esther 5:4 *And Esther answered, If it seem good unto the king, let the king and Haman come this day unto the banquet that I have prepared for him.*

Esther has been offered "half of the kingdom." She has been given a blank check. The king is sitting there waiting to hear what huge, expensive thing she is going to ask for. And when she asks, what she asks for is... "I want you and Haman to come to a feast that I have prepared for you. I just knew you'd say yes, so I went ahead and fixed it!"

There are two things that leap out at me. Number one, she is offered so much but satisfied with so little. Learn from that. Be a person who doesn't have to have much in order to be satisfied. If you are like that, you will be a priceless jewel to your spouse one day.

The second thing I notice, though, is her mystery and intrigue. She clearly understands the power of a mysterious woman. She didn't tell him what the feast was for! She didn't tell him why Haman needed to be there! She had just showed up, unannounced, and taken over his day. And look how he responded.

Esther 5:5 *Then the king said, Cause Haman to make haste, that he may do as Esther hath said. So the king and Haman came to the banquet that Esther had prepared.*

He didn't say, "Well, ok, I guess I can fit in in, say, around 8:00ish. Let me check with Haman and see if that fits in his schedule, and I'll get back to you." No, he said,

"Somebody get Haman, RIGHT NOW, and tell him we have a dinner to go to. Tell him to drop whatever he is doing, and come immediately!"

Esther has got his curiosity piqued! He is being reminded all over again why he chose this woman as his new queen over all of the other beauties in the Persian Empire!

Esther went to her chambers, got everything set up, and almost immediately, the king and Haman arrived. They had their feast, and it came time to get down to business.

Esther 5:6 *And the king said unto Esther at the banquet of wine, What is thy petition? and it shall be granted thee: and what is thy request? even to the half of the kingdom it shall be performed.*

Ahasuerus is in a really good mood. Ladies, an interruption to a man's day is often a very good thing! He asks her again, this time in the presence of Haman, what she wants. He once again hands her the second blank check as before.

And this time she answers:

Esther 5:7 *Then answered Esther, and said, My petition and my request is; 8 If I have found favour in the sight of the king, and if it please the king to grant my petition, and to perform my request, let the king and Haman come to the banquet that I shall prepare for them, and I will do to morrow as the king hath said.*

Another layer of mystery and anticipation! She comes within just a word of actually telling him what she wants, and then says, "Tell you what. Both of you come back tomorrow, and I promise you I'll ask for it then."

The king loves this. He is getting to look like the biggest, coolest kid on the block in front of his buddy Haman!

He is getting chased by his wife in front of his VP. Haman loves it too, as we will see in the following verses. In fact, Haman loves it just like a great big bass loves it when he is swimming along, minding his own business, and he suddenly hears the thrashing and wriggling of a big, fat, juicy worm in the water that seems to have appeared out of nowhere.

The Will of Mordecai
Esther 5:9 *Then went Haman forth that day joyful and with a glad heart: but when Haman saw Mordecai in the king's gate, that he stood not up, nor moved for him, he was full of indignation against Mordecai.*

There are some great heroes in Scripture, men who did amazing things for God. But I am just as much or more fascinated by some of the lesser known heroes of the Bible. For me, Mordecai fits that description. Mordecai got into all kind of trouble with Haman, the VP of the Persian Empire. He got into trouble for refusing to bow his face to the ground and worship Haman. As a result, Haman put a plan into motion that was going to destroy every Jew in the world, including, *especially rather,* Mordecai.

How, I wonder, would we respond to Haman after that? After all, if he has the power to order our death, maybe he will also be willing to spare our lives! Maybe if we apologize to him, maybe if we bow down and kiss his feet, maybe if we cry giant crocodile tears, maybe if we apologize and promise to bow before him every day from now on, maybe he will forgive us!

Not Mordecai. This man did not have a reverse gear. To Mordecai, right was always right. Not only was he not going to bow, he actually determined to take it even a step further. The text says that he would not stand up–or move! That tells me that he was sitting...right in the way that Haman had to walk on the way home! If he wasn't in the way, he wouldn't have needed to move. It seems that he actually sat right there, glaring at Haman and making Haman ease his way around him.

Some people deserve no respect whatsoever, and Haman qualified.

That absolutely wrecked Haman's day. He had been on top of the world, riding on clouds, the only person other than the king himself invited into the feast with the queen, the only person invited back the next day, things were fabulous...and then he ran right into Mordecai.

Why couldn't Mordecai just play nice and go along to get along? I'll tell you why: he had a will to do right. Doing right was more important to him than getting along. Doing right was more important than being popular. Doing right was even more important than staying alive!

The Weaknesses of Haman

Esther 5:10 *Nevertheless Haman refrained himself: and when he came home, he sent and called for his friends, and Zeresh his wife.* **11** *And Haman told them of the glory of his riches, and the multitude of his children, and all the things wherein the king had promoted him, and how he had advanced him above the princes and servants of the king.* **12** *Haman said moreover, Yea, Esther the queen did let no man come in with the king unto the banquet that she had prepared but* *myself; and to morrow am I invited unto her also with the king.*

There is not much explanation necessary about what Haman did and said in these verses. Simply put, he was bragging. In fact, he didn't just brag to those who he happened to come in contact with, he actually called a bunch of friends over to his house for the specific purpose of bragging to them about how great he was!

Can you imagine such a thing? Can you imagine having someone call you over to their house along with a bunch of other buddies and saying, "Now everyone sit down right here in the living room. I want us all to talk for a while about a very important subject. ME!

"I wanted you all to know that first of all, I am rich. Are you all having trouble paying any of your bills? Man, that's too bad. I just pay all of mine off as soon as they come in. In fact, I'm four or five months ahead on all my bills. We never eat at home; every night is Outback for us. I'm thinking of trading in the Mercedes on a Bentley or two.

"Gee, I wonder what time it is. Let me check my 18 carat gold, diamond encrusted Rolex: looks like it's 'Haman time!'

"I am pretty. I have pretty kids. I'm so popular that Facebook is about to change its name to 'Hamanbook.' Oh and by the way, I have all of you guy's Christmas gifts early this year: I have an autographed 8x10 of me, for you.

"No, no, no, don't cry, I understand. My greatness overwhelms you. I get it, sometimes I even overwhelm myself. I mean, I personally don't think I'm anything special, but who am I to argue with the 6.6 billion other people on Earth who would do anything to be me?"

Haman had a weakness, friends. His weakness was that he was wildly, madly in love... with himself. He was proud, haughty, and arrogant. And what does the Bible say about that kind of pride?

Proverbs 16:18 *Pride goeth before destruction, and an haughty spirit before a fall.*

Haman was about to experience the truth of this verse. In addition to his pride, Haman had another weakness, and that was that he couldn't be happy with **anything** unless he had **everything**. Look at the next verse.

Esther 5:13 *Yet all this availeth me nothing, so long as I see Mordecai the Jew sitting at the king's gate.*

Haman has just admitted to being filthy rich, having a bunch of kids, being popular, being married, having great contacts in high places, and the conclusion to all of it is that none of it even matters as long as one old man that he doesn't like is still around!

This probably won't surprise you, but that still didn't exhaust the list of his weaknesses. There was yet another and it would prove to be a fatal one.

Esther 5:14 *Then said Zeresh his wife and all his friends unto him, Let a gallows be made of fifty cubits high, and to morrow speak thou unto the king that Mordecai may be hanged thereon: then go thou in merrily with the king unto the banquet. And the thing pleased Haman; and he caused the gallows to be made.*

What weakness was demonstrated here? The weakness of relying on poor counselors. The advice they gave him was absolutely terrible, and he loved it.

What kind of a wife thinks this way? She takes the lead; she is the first one mentioned as suggesting that her husband build a 75 foot tall gallows to hang an old man on! She then said, "After you've hung the old man, Sweetie, just go on to your party with the king and queen and have a great time. Oh, and how about bringing me home some vanilla from the marketplace?"

These people had no heart, no conscience, nothing. Before the night was done, there was a 75 foot tall gallows built right there in Haman's yard. That kind of thing could not be missed by anyone. Haman knew who it was for. His wife and friends knew who it was for. The king's chamberlains knew who it was for. Mordecai definitely knew who it was for. But here is the thing: the 75 foot gallows was not nearly as important as that fat, juicy worm, wiggling on Esther's hook that Haman had already swallowed—hook, line, and sinker.

Chapter 6
A Case of Divine Insomnia

Esther 6:1 *On that night could not the king sleep, and he commanded to bring the book of records of the chronicles; and they were read before the king. 2 And it was found written, that Mordecai had told of Bigthana and Teresh, two of the king's chamberlains, the keepers of the door, who sought to lay hand on the king Ahasuerus. 3 And the king said, What honour and dignity hath been done to Mordecai for this? Then said the king's servants that ministered unto him, There is nothing done for him. 4 And the king said, Who is in the court? Now Haman was come into the outward court of the king's house, to speak unto the king to hang Mordecai on the gallows that he had prepared for him. 5 And the king's servants said unto him, Behold, Haman standeth in the court. And the king said, Let him come in. 6 So Haman came in. And the king said unto him, What shall be done unto the man whom the king delighteth to honour? Now Haman thought in his heart, To whom would the king delight to do honour more than to myself? 7 And Haman answered the king, For the man whom the king delighteth to honour, 8 Let the royal apparel be brought which the king useth to wear, and the horse that the king rideth upon, and the crown royal which is set upon his* *head:* **9** *And let this apparel and horse be delivered to the hand of one of the king's most noble princes, that they may array the man withal whom the king delighteth to honour, and bring him on horseback through the street of the city, and proclaim before him, Thus shall it be done to the man whom the king delighteth to honour.* **10** *Then the king said to Haman, Make haste, and take the apparel and the horse, as thou hast said, and do even so to Mordecai the Jew, that sitteth at the king's gate: let nothing fail of all that thou hast spoken.* **11** *Then took Haman the apparel and the horse, and arrayed Mordecai, and brought him on horseback through the street of the city, and proclaimed before him, Thus shall it be done unto the man whom the king delighteth to honour.* **12** *And Mordecai came again to the king's gate. But Haman hasted to his house mourning, and having his head covered.* **13** *And Haman told Zeresh his wife and all his friends every thing that had befallen him. Then said his wise men and Zeresh his wife unto him, If Mordecai be of the seed of the Jews, before whom thou hast begun to fall, thou shalt not prevail against him, but shalt surely fall before him.* **14** *And while they were yet talking with him, came the king's chamberlains, and hasted to bring Haman unto the banquet that Esther had prepared.*

There are many times in life when timing is everything...

God's timing is something that we often question and very often doubt. We know that Martha and Mary doubted His timing when Jesus showed up four days after their brother, Lazarus, died. We have often doubted His timing when the due date for a bill comes and goes with no means to pay it. We certainly doubt His timing when a child or a teenager passes away: we feel like that young person surely should have been allowed to live a full life, grow old, and then die. We question His timing when we lose our jobs right at the time when, for some reason, the family bills have just increased. We doubt God's timing a lot.

I have no doubt in my mind that Esther and Mordecai and the Jews doubted His timing a lot during the time of the events of the book of Esther. But chapter six of the book of Esther is conclusive proof that the timing of God is perfect.

A Sleepless Night

Esther 6:1 *On that night could not the king sleep, and he commanded to bring the book of records of the chronicles; and they were read before the king.* **2** *And it was found written, that Mordecai had told of Bigthana and Teresh, two of the king's chamberlains, the keepers of the door, who sought to lay hand on the king Ahasuerus.*

On **that** night...

Ahasuerus was a fully grown man. He was old enough to have married, waged wars, had victories, and experienced defeats. Since the time he was a baby, he had done like every other human on earth: he had lived and functioned through the day and then gone to bed and gone to sleep. But on this particular night, that pattern was interrupted. I am guessing that he was like all of us; for the most part, we have no trouble sleeping, but every once in a great while we find ourselves unable to go to sleep at night. There is not much of any significance to us when that happens. But on this night and with this king, it was very significant. You see, this was very clearly not a case of natural insomnia but a case of divine insomnia. There could not have been a more perfect night at all for this king to not be able to sleep.

Hours earlier, wicked Haman had been bragging to his wife and friends about all of his greatness and glory. Then he began to whine about one old man, Mordecai, who would not bow down to him. His wife and friends made the brilliant suggestion that he build a gallows fifty cubits high and hang the old man on it. Immediately he commissioned the work and had the workers start right then and there cutting boards and driving nails. It didn't have to be pretty; it just had to be functional.

It was clearly some time either near to dark or it may have actually already been dark. My guess is they had to finish this project by lamp light. Do you know what I cannot help but wonder? I cannot help but wonder whether or not God allowed every pop of the hammer to actually make it to the ears of the king. The king's chamberlains knew about this, so it had to be somewhere near to the palace! Maybe while Ahasuerus tried to sleep he was hearing a faint "Whap! Whap! Whap!" from somewhere in the distance.

One way or another, it was on that very night, that most important night, which the king could not sleep. This was absolutely God at work.

The king wanted sleep, badly. So he did what we often do when we need sleep; he picked out some reading material. In this case, he asked for the Chronicles of the Kings to be read before him. Do you remember the books of Chronicles in the Bible? The Chronicle books of all ancient kings were very much like them. They would have a whole lot of "so and so begat so and so, begat so and so, begat so and so, begat so and so," and then every now and then there would be a little interesting tidbit of information thrown in.

I am not too pious to admit this: if I really need sleep, I am reading the books of the Chronicles rather than the book of the Revelation!

Ahasuerus tossed and turned and finally got somebody to bring in the books of the Chronicles and read it out loud to him. That had to sound a whole lot like the humming of a florescent light ballast. But somewhere in the midst of all of the endless droning of "begat, begat, begat," something caught the king's ear, causing him to sit straight up and take notice, something that was not just recorded in that book of Chronicles but also in what would later become the Biblical book of Esther.

Esther 2:21 *In those days, while Mordecai sat in the king's gate, two of the king's chamberlains, Bigthan and Teresh, of those which kept the door, were wroth, and sought to lay hand on the king Ahasuerus.* **22** *And the thing was known to Mordecai, who told it unto Esther the queen; and Esther certified the king thereof in Mordecai's name.* **23** *And when inquisition was made of the matter, it was found out; therefore they were both hanged on a tree: and it was written in the book of the chronicles before the king.*

That is what was read to the king on the night that he was trying to get bored enough to go to sleep! Needless to say, it had the exact opposite effect! And then, for some reason, the king asked a question...

A Shocking Oversight

Esther 6:3 *And the king said, What honour and dignity hath been done to Mordecai for this? Then said the king's servants that ministered unto him, There is nothing done for him.*

This was an oversight of the highest order. An Oriental monarch would be horrified at the realization that one of his subjects had done something so great for him and that he had neglected to reward him.

And that brings us right back to that perfect timing of God, and that also brings up a worthwhile rabbit trail to pursue concerning the expectations of man. Was Mordecai a human being or not? Certainly, he was. As a human being, the thought had to have occurred to him at least once, and probably very many times, truth be told, that he had been done wrong. He had done a great thing and had not been rewarded in the least.

Who would be the two people that he would be most prone to blame? Well, the king is an obvious choice. The king had his life saved; he was in a position to reward Mordecai for that great service, and yet, had not done so. In fact, he had gone so far as to forget all about it!

I have learned that I really should not be surprised at the ability of people to forget very great things that they have done for them. I have been alive for 42 years now (and pastoring for 15 of those years), and I have often had to shake my head at this. I remember sitting in my office and getting a phone call from a lady that my wife and I had sacrificed in enormous ways to help. That lady that we had done so much for over, and over, and over, and over again proceeded to rip into me and say the most vile and hateful and untrue things. I cried. It hurt so bad to realize that she clearly did not remember one thing we had ever done for her. People are great at forgetting things that people have done for them. This happened with Mordecai. The king forgot what he did for him.

But there was a second person that Mordecai would be prone to blame and that was God. Mordecai was human. And do you know what Christian humans almost always do in a situation like this? We get a case of the mullygrubs against God: *God, it isn't fair! I saved this man's life, and he doesn't even remember! I can maybe understand how he would forget, but not You. You are God! If anybody should have remembered and rewarded me, You should have. God, what are you doing?*

Be honest; haven't there been times in your own life where you felt a lot like that? You see, this was an oversight by Ahasuerus, but this was intentional where God was concerned. In fact, I will tell you point blank that I am certain that God Himself was the One behind Ahasuerus forgetting. God needed for Ahasuerus to forget back then so that God could bring it back to his attention at just the exact, perfect time.

A Superb Timing

Esther 6:4 *And the king said, Who is in the court? Now Haman was come into the outward court of the king's house, to speak unto the king to hang Mordecai on the gallows that he had prepared for him.*

Please, follow the timing of all of this very carefully. The king is trying to sleep, so we are dealing with the night-time hours. He has been given a case of divine insomnia. But he isn't the only one that cannot sleep that night. Haman can't sleep either. He is so enraged at Mordecai, and so pleased at the thought of hanging him, that he is still awake too! So, since he is awake, he reasons that he may as well go on into the outer court and wait for the first available opportunity to speak to the king. He doesn't care if he has to wait for hours: he wants to make sure that he is the first person in line to speak to the king when he is up and around.

But the king is already up and around. He is pacing the floor, really upset at the oversight of not having done anything for Mordecai. He looks up at an attendant and says, "Who is in the court? Who is out there? I need some really quick advice. Surely somebody worthwhile must also be awake right now. Is anybody out there?"

And the attendant says, "You're in luck, O King. Not only is someone out there, but it is your favorite someone! Haman, your most trusted advisor, the guy that you let write laws in your name with your ring, he is in the court!"

The Bible tells us why he was there. He was there to get permission from the king to hang Mordecai. But the king didn't know that. And what's more, he didn't ask. He was so consumed with his own thoughts that he really didn't care why Haman had come: he just wanted to get some input from him on his own issue.

Esther 6:5 *And the king's servants said unto him, Behold, Haman standeth in the court. And the king said, Let him come in.*

Haman was expecting to have to ask for permission to see the king. But now, suddenly, as if by a "stroke of luck," he is issued in before the king on the spot! He had to have felt like there was some divine intervention going on at that moment! And there was! Only, he didn't realize that divine intervention was not on his behalf, it was on Mordecai's behalf.

A Stunning Reversal

Please, bear in mind that up to this point in the book absolutely everything has been coming up roses for Haman. He had been on a lucky streak that would make a Las Vegas gambler the richest man on Earth. Nothing, NOTHING has gone wrong for him, and as far as he knows, absolutely everything has gone wrong for his enemies. It is the start of the fourth quarter of the Super Bowl, and he is winning 50-0 and has the ball. But Haman was about to experience the greatest turn of events that Earth has ever seen.

Esther 6:6 *So Haman came in. And the king said unto him, What shall be done unto the man whom the king delighteth to honour? Now Haman thought in his heart, To whom would the king delight to do honour more than to myself?*

I cannot begin to fully describe the depth of arrogance that Haman demonstrated in this verse. The Persian Empire was by most estimates 100 million strong. And when the king asks Haman what should be done to the man that the king delighted to honor, his first thought was, "It must be me! There are 100 million people in the empire, and the king wants to honor someone, so obviously, it is me!

"2, 4, 6, 8, who does he appreciate? Me! Me! Me, Me, Me!

"Ladies and gentlemen: in this corner, standing five foot five, 130 pounds, with a head the size of a large pumpkin, the marvelous, the magnificent, the MAN... HAYYYYYYYYYYYYYYYYMAN!"

This guy was so full of himself there wasn't room for air.

Esther 6:7 *And Haman answered the king, For the man whom the king delighteth to honour,* **8** *Let the royal apparel be brought which the king useth to wear, and the horse that the king rideth upon, and the crown royal which is set upon his head:* **9** *And let this apparel and horse be delivered to the hand of one of the king's most noble princes, that they may array the man withal whom the king delighteth to honour, and bring him on horseback through the street of the city, and proclaim before him, Thus shall it be done to the man whom the king delighteth to honour.*

The irony in these verses is truly beautiful. If Haman had thought that there was any possibility that anyone at all other than himself was in the king's mind, he would have suggested a far more humble and far less sizable reward. Not just Mordecai, *anybody*. As far as Haman was concerned, no one at all could ever be worthy of such a thing as this other than himself.

These ceremonies where a royal personage was brought through the streets in honor were not quick ceremonies. They usually took hours and hours.[18] Haman is intent on making his reward something very memorable and very long lasting.

Haman in this passage shows the exact same desire as someone else in Scripture is shown as having.

Isaiah 14:12 *How art thou fallen from heaven, O Lucifer, son of the morning! how art thou cut down to the ground, which didst weaken the nations!* **13** *For thou hast said in thine heart, I will ascend into heaven, I will exalt my throne above the stars of God: I will sit also upon the mount of the congregation, in the sides of the north:* **14** *I will ascend above the heights of the clouds; I will be like the most High.*

What Haman wanted in these verses is exactly what the devil wanted! The devil wanted to have the position and prestige that belonged to his rightful King, and Haman wanted to have the position and prestige that belonged to his rightful king. In both cases, this was the grievous sin of pride. And just like it caused the downfall of Satan, it was also going to cause the downfall of Haman.

Haman had delivered his advice. He had instructed the king on what the king should do for him, uh, I mean, what the king should do for "the one he delights to honor," wink wink, nudge nudge...

Esther 6:10 *Then the king said to Haman, Make haste, and take the apparel and the horse, as thou hast said, and do even so to Mordecai the Jew, that sitteth at the king's gate: let nothing fail of all that thou hast spoken.*

Can we take just a moment and savor this? This, friends, is like a really good steak or a big juicy lobster; it is something that you don't want to gobble down. You just want to taste it, feel the texture, chew it slowly, one delicious bit at a time.

Can you imagine the look on Haman's face? Go ahead, try and see it in your mind. Can you imagine that awful, sinking feeling in his stomach? Can you grasp what it was like for him to try and hide what he was feeling from the king at that moment? *Yes, Your Majesty, your will is my command, Your Majesty, with pleasure, Your Majesty...*

That scene had to have all of Heaven laughing hysterically!

Now, please, let me clear one thing up for you. You might at this point be wondering why the king would honor a man that he knew was a Jew, when he had already given permission for all of the Jews to be killed. Please, look back with me at the exact words that Haman said to the king when he proposed this slaughter, and you will find your answer.

Esther 3:8 *And Haman said unto king Ahasuerus, There is a certain people scattered abroad and dispersed among the people in all the provinces of thy kingdom; and their laws are diverse from all people; neither keep they the king's laws: therefore it is not for the king's profit to suffer them. **9** If it please the king, let it be written that they may be destroyed: and I will pay ten thousand talents of silver to the hands of those that have the charge of the business, to bring it into the king's treasuries.*

What do you notice in this? Haman never told the king who the people were that were to be destroyed! The king agreed to this destruction without even being told who the decree would say was to be killed. By the time of chapter six, he still doesn't know. So when he chose to honor Mordecai the Jew, he had no idea that he was honoring someone whose death warrant he had already given Haman permission to sign for him.

Haman had his command. *Go and honor Mordecai the Jew in the exact manner you just described, don't leave anything out*. And that brings us to what I see as another hilarious episode in this book.

Esther 6:11 *Then took Haman the apparel and the horse, and arrayed Mordecai, and brought him on horseback through the street of the city, and proclaimed before him, Thus shall it be done unto the man whom the king delighteth to honour.*

What I find hilarious in this particular verse is what this all must have been like for Mordecai! Mordecai is used to Haman growling and glaring at him. Mordecai knows that Haman has just built a 75 foot tall gallows to hang him on. Mordecai sees Haman coming his way, and he has to be thinking *Well, Elizabeth, this is it! This is the big one!* But then Haman stops in front of him... his hands are shaking... his eyes are bloodshot... and he says, "Mordecai! By the command of the great King Ahasuerus, you are to be arrayed in the royal garments, you are to be placed on the royal horse, you are to wear the royal crown, and you are to be honored throughout the streets of the city!"

A few minutes later, the old man is riding on the royal horse, wearing the king's crown, clothed in the king's royal garments, and being led through the street. Leading his horse is a man who is shouting out over and over again, "Thus shall it be done to the man whom the king delights to honor!" And the best part is that the man having to do all that shouting is Haman himself! And you tell me that God doesn't have a sense of humor? I would pay big money to have been able to see all of that!

Do you know, though, what the sad part of all of this is? The fact that Haman himself was being honored by all of this and was too proud to realize it. See if you can figure out why I say that Haman was being honored by it. Here is the answer.

Esther 6:7 *And Haman answered the king, For the man whom the king delighteth to honour, **8** Let the royal apparel be brought which the king useth to wear, and the horse that the king rideth upon, and the crown royal which is set upon his head: **9** And let this apparel and horse be delivered to the hand of **one of the king's most noble princes**, that they may array the man withal whom the king delighteth to honour, and bring him on horseback through the street of the city, and proclaim before him, Thus shall it be done to the man whom the king delighteth to honour. **10** Then the king said to Haman, Make haste, **and take the apparel and the horse, as thou hast said, and do even so** to Mordecai the Jew, that sitteth at the king's gate: let nothing fail of all that thou hast spoken.*

Do you see that? Haman said, "Let one of your most noble princes do all of this."

And the king said, "Great idea, go do it!"

The king just proclaimed Haman to be one of his most noble princes! Now, yes, that shows that the king had poor judgment, but that is not the point. The point is that Haman should have been honored, but his pride made it to where an honor done to him was regarded as a humiliation done to him. If you are a proud person, things that ought to seem wonderful to you will end up seeming terrible to you, because you are too big and important in your own eyes to realize just how nice people are being to you.

Esther 6:12 *And Mordecai came again to the king's gate. But Haman hasted to his house mourning, and having his head covered.*

The contrast between these two men could not be more clearly seen than it is in this verse. Mordecai has a huge honor done to him, but when it is done, he goes right back to his place and right back to being who he has always been. But Haman has a huge honor done to him, and when it is done, he goes home with his face and head covered up in shame. This has been the most shocking of reversals for him. This night has not gone anything at all like he thought. God has stepped in, and everything has turned on a dime. God is very good about things like that. But there is yet one more little aspect to this bad, bad, terrible, bad, not so very good night for Haman.

Esther 6:13 *And Haman told Zeresh his wife and all his friends every thing that had befallen him. Then said his wise men and Zeresh his wife unto him, If Mordecai be of the seed of the Jews, before whom thou hast begun to fall, thou shalt not prevail against him, but shalt surely fall before him.*

Wait just a minute: does anyone remember who it was that suggested that Haman build the gallows and hang Mordecai? That would be his wife and friends. Now these very same friends are going, "Dude, this is bad. You are like, toast, Dude, and Mordecai is the toaster. It must stink to be you!"

Be warned: people will be very good at getting you into trouble and then they will back off and leave you hanging when it all goes bad for you! You might want to refrain from listening to people who are constantly stirring you up and getting you into fights and arguments that they themselves are too chicken to get into for themselves. Have you ever played chess? If so, you may have noticed that the pawns tend to get killed with alarming regularity, while the big boys stay safely behind them. A lot of people are too foolish to realize that other people are using them as pawns and that it isn't going to end well for them.

A Summons to Dinner

Esther 6:14 *And while they were yet talking with him, came the king's chamberlains, and hasted to bring Haman unto the banquet that Esther had prepared.*

I believe that the fact that these men had to come and get Haman gives us a window into his emotions at that point. Everything about Haman up until this point in the book tells us that his natural propensity would be to have been already waiting in the court for the opportunity to come in. But he is now so disjointed, so torn up inside, the chamberlains have to come to his house and get him. It is almost as if when it was time for the banquet the attendants looked around and said, "Where's Haman? It isn't like him not to already be here! Somebody send someone after him; the king and queen are ready!"

May I tell you something? Haman was in no mood to go to a dinner party right then. His entire world has just been turned upside down. All he wants to do is go to his bedroom, crawl under the covers, pull them up over his head, and have someone sing, *"Make the world go away... and get it off my shoulders..."*

But you see, he didn't have a choice in the matter. Haman had exactly one choice in the book of Esther. He got to choose whether he would defy God or not, in this case, by coming against God's people. And may I tell you that this is the exact same choice that we have? We get to decide whether to obey or disobey God. Once that decision is made, the train has left the station, and it is going to stop when and where the Conductor intends for it to stop, even if you are under it.

Throughout this book people made choices, and God then settled the matter.

Proverbs 16:9 *A man's heart deviseth his way: but the LORD directeth his steps.*

For good or bad, this verse is true. You make decisions, good or bad, and then God brings the results based on those decisions. The New Testament famously put it this way:

Galatians 6:7 *Be not deceived; God is not mocked: for whatsoever a man soweth, that shall he also reap.*

Mordecai sowed right. Mordecai obeyed God even when it was not popular. And then God stepped in and took over for him with shocking and pleasant results. One minute he was at the gate waiting to be hung and the next minute he was being led through the street in honor by the man who wanted to hang him. Mordecai didn't do that; God did that.

Haman sowed wrong. Haman disobeyed God. Then God stepped in and took over for him with shocking and unpleasant results. One minute he was waiting to see the king to get permission to hang Mordecai and the next minute he was completely humiliated, leading Mordecai through the streets in honor.

Do you know what all of this tells us? From the divine insomnia that the king experienced on just the right night, to the fact that someone read to the king the exact spot in the huge Chronicles of the Kings of Persia where it told of Mordecai saving his life, to the fact that Haman ended up in the court at that exact moment, it tells us that God is in

111

control! He may not always make it so obvious, in fact, I would say that He rarely makes it quite so obvious, but He is in control nonetheless. We are serving the same God that Esther and Mordecai served. Next time things seem to be falling apart in your life, remember that, and just keep doing right! His timing is not likely to be the same as our timing, but His timing is always perfect.

Chapter 7
Oh, What a Tangled Web We Weave...

Esther 7:1 *So the king and Haman came to banquet with Esther the queen. 2 And the king said again unto Esther on the second day at the banquet of wine, What is thy petition, queen Esther? and it shall be granted thee: and what is thy request? and it shall be performed, even to the half of the kingdom. 3 Then Esther the queen answered and said, If I have found favour in thy sight, O king, and if it please the king, let my life be given me at my petition, and my people at my request: 4 For we are sold, I and my people, to be destroyed, to be slain, and to perish. But if we had been sold for bondmen and bondwomen, I had held my tongue, although the enemy could not countervail the king's damage. 5 Then the king Ahasuerus answered and said unto Esther the queen, Who is he, and where is he, that durst presume in his heart to do so? 6 And Esther said, The adversary and enemy is this wicked Haman. Then Haman was afraid before the king and the queen. 7 And the king arising from the banquet of wine in his wrath went into the palace garden: and Haman stood up to make request for his life to Esther the queen; for he saw that there was evil determined against him by the king. 8 Then the king returned out of the palace garden into the place of the* *banquet of wine; and Haman was fallen upon the bed whereon Esther was. Then said the king, Will he force the queen also before me in the house? As the word went out of the king's mouth, they covered Haman's face. 9 And Harbonah, one of the chamberlains, said before the king, Behold also, the gallows fifty cubits high, which Haman had made for Mordecai, who had spoken good for the king, standeth in the house of Haman. Then the king said, Hang him thereon. 10 So they hanged Haman on the gallows that he had prepared for Mordecai. Then was the king's wrath pacified.*

In chapter six everything began to unravel for Haman on a personal level. He came to the conclusion that he was going to end up spending his life having to endure Mordecai being around to torment him. But you and I know now what he did not know then; things were actually much worse for him than he even realized! He had raised his hands against God's people, and God was going to destroy him.

A Three-Fold Promise

Esther 7:1 *So the king and Haman came to banquet with Esther the queen. 2 And the king said again unto Esther on the second day at the banquet of wine, What is thy petition, queen Esther? and it shall be granted thee: and what is thy request? and it shall be performed, even to the half of the kingdom.*

It is now five to six days after the decree went out to destroy the Jews. Haman issued the decree, then there were three days of fasting that the Jews aware of the situation engaged in, then there was two days of Esther wooing the king. The day before, she had walked un-invited into the king's presence knowing that it could mean the end of her life. She had found grace in the eyes of the king, and he had extended the royal scepter to her, sparing her life.

At that point he made her a promise. Whatever she wanted, even to half of his kingdom, he would give it to her. So she requested a little thing, a thing of mystery and intrigue. She asked for the king and Haman to come to a banquet that she had prepared for them, and they did. At that banquet, he once again offered to give her anything, even up to half of the kingdom. Haman was there to hear that promise. Once again, she goes mysterious, asking for the two of them to come back the next day for yet another banquet and promising to reveal her request at that one.

The next day the three of them are gathered together yet again. This time Haman is not in a good mood. His world has been unraveling, and he likely thinks that things could not possibly get any worse. He is wrong.

At that banquet, the king for a third time offers to give Esther anything she wants, even up to half of the kingdom. Haman has got to be a bit amazed at just how deeply the king seems to love and appreciate this woman. Esther is clearly a woman that owns the king's heart and affections. For a promise like this to be made even once is amazing, for it to be made twice is jaw-dropping, for it to be made three separate times is earth-shattering.

This should give you a small hint as to how deeply Christ loves His bride. When you see how many times in Scripture He repeats the same promises to us over and over and over: promises to return for us, promises never to leave or forsake us, promises to provide for us, promises to hear us when we pray, you must know that He loves us. The Lord loves us, His bride, dearly!

Just like Esther, we often find ourselves clinging to His promises during some very troubling times. Esther was carrying the weight of the world on her slender shoulders, and she was about to grab hold of those promises like a drowning man grabs for a lifeline.

A Tearful Plea

Esther 7:3 *Then Esther the queen answered and said, If I have found favour in thy sight, O king, and if it please the king, let my life be given me at my petition, and my people at my request:* **4a** *For we are sold, I and my people, to be destroyed, to be slain, and to perish.*

You could blindfold yourself, plug up your ears, walk out onto Highway 74, get hit by a Mack truck doing 80mph, and it would not be any more of a shock to you than the shock Haman just experienced in these verses. He just got blind sided, steam rolled, pick your adjective, he never saw this one coming.

Sweet Esther, apple of the king's eye, the woman that has wooed him with mystery for the last two days, turns to the king in the presence of Haman and delivers her request. She has been offered anything at all that she wants. And what does she ask for? "My dear husband, my king, all I want is for my life to be spared and that of my people. I am going to be murdered unless you do something. Would you please save me from the man who wants to kill me?"

The man she is asking this of is Ahasuerus, Xerxes. This is the man of the incredibly hot temper and unbelievably short fuse. This is the man that for absolutely no good reason cut a man's son in half and marched his army between the two pieces of his dead body. This man's wife is asking for her husband to save her and her people from a murderer.

Oh, by the way, even though she had not mentioned the fact that she was a Jew, Haman knew exactly who and what she was talking about. How? She used the exact wording of his decree against them! In English it sounds almost identical:

Esther 3:13 *And the letters were sent by posts into all the king's provinces, **to destroy, to kill**, and **to cause to perish**, all Jews, both young and old, little children and women, in one day, even upon the thirteenth day of the twelfth month, which is the month Adar, and to take the spoil of them for a prey.*

Esther 7:4 *For we are sold, I and my people, **to be destroyed, to be slain**, and **to perish**. But if we had been sold for bondmen and bondwomen, I had held my tongue, although the enemy could not countervail the king's damage.*

It is nearly identical in English. It is completely word for word identical in Hebrew. She quoted the exact words of Haman's decree right there in the presence of the king. Can you imagine the horrible, heart-sinking feeling Haman had at that moment? And now the wisdom of Mordecai becomes clear! Mordecai had told Esther back in chapter two verse ten not to tell anyone that she was a Jew. When Haman issued the decree he had no idea of what race the queen was. But now, when it matters most, she is going to pull that ace out of her sleeve.

Look at the last half of verse four with me and notice one more thing about sweet Esther before we move forward.

Esther 7:4b *...But if we had been sold for bondmen and bondwomen, I had held my tongue, although the enemy could not countervail the king's damage.*

She was saying, "My husband, if we had just been consigned to become slaves; if all that was going to happen to me was that I was going to lose my crown and become a slave on the auction block in the market, I wouldn't have even bothered you about all of this, even though I know that the enemy could never stand against you if you should choose to act."

That is one sweet-spirited woman. Her beauty attracted the king to her, but her spirit kept him in love with her. Ladies, you need to remember that.

A Terrifying Point

Esther 7:5 *Then the king Ahasuerus answered and said unto Esther the queen, Who is he, and where is he, that durst presume in his heart to do so? 6 And Esther said, The adversary and enemy is this wicked Haman. Then Haman was afraid before the king and the queen.*

Other than the guards, there were three principle people in that room. There were two proud men, the king and Haman, and there was one sweet little woman, Esther. Of the three, do you realize that only one of them, only Esther, knew everything that was going on?

The king knew that Haman had issued a decree to destroy a "certain people." But he did not know that the certain people were the Jews, and he did not know that Esther, his wife, was a Jew. Haman knew that he had issued a decree to destroy the Jews, he knew that Mordecai was a Jew, but he did not know that Queen Esther was a Jew, nor did he know that Mordecai was related to Esther and had raised her like a daughter after her parents died.

In that room, only Esther knew all of this, and Esther was ready to talk. When the king in rage asked who the would-be murderer was, Esther pointed right into the face of the king's most trusted counselor and said, "That's him!"

Notice also that she called him "that wicked Haman." I find that refreshing. In our day, the one snippet of Scripture that everyone seems to remember is "judge not!" They cannot tell you where it is or to whom it was written or what the context of the verse is, but they firmly believe that you can never take a stand against anything that anyone is doing, for if you do, you are violating the "judge not" clause of Scripture.

For the record, here is that phrase **Matthew 7:1** *Judge not, that ye be not judged.*

That sounds pretty conclusive, doesn't it? But why don't we look at the entire passage for a moment.

Matthew 7:1 *Judge not, that ye be not judged.* **2** *For with what judgment ye judge, ye shall be judged: and with what measure ye mete, it shall be measured to you again.* **3** *And why beholdest thou the mote that is in thy brother's eye, but considerest not the beam that is in thine own eye?* **4** *Or how wilt thou say to thy brother, Let me pull out the mote out of thine eye; and, behold, a beam is in thine own eye?* **5** *Thou hypocrite, first cast out the beam out of thine own eye; and then shalt thou see clearly to cast out the mote out of thy brother's eye.*

Do you understand that passage? It was written to hypocrites according to verse five. It was written to people who lived wicked lives yet complained about far less wickedness in others. That kind of a person is not allowed to judge. A child molester is not allowed to judge a jaywalker. A rapist is not allowed to judge someone who runs a stop sign. A drunk is not allowed to judge a litterbug. A person with a giant beam in his eye is not allowed to judge someone with a tiny speck of dirt in his eye. He is to get the beam out first, and then he is qualified to make a judgment along the lines of, "Oh look! You have a speck of dirt in your eye; let me help get it out." That is what this passage teaches.

But that is not all the Bible teaches about judging:

Luke 12:57 *Yea, and why even of yourselves judge ye not what is right?*

This was Jesus asking people why they weren't judging! There were things that were wrong, things that were right, and He was asking them why they were not making proper judgment calls on those issues.

John 7:24 *Judge not according to the appearance, **but judge righteous judgment**.*

This is a command to judge. Not a suggestion, not a good idea, a command. We are told in this passage to look beyond the surface of issues, root through things carefully, and then make a righteous judgment on whatever it is we are facing.

Matthew 7:20 *Wherefore by their fruits ye shall know them.*

This verse, also from the mouth of Jesus, tells us that we can know whether people are good or bad by what they do. What is that? Judging! We are certainly to refrain from being people that spend our time looking for ways to put down and criticize others, but we are most assuredly to be people that can and do openly distinguish between right and wrong. The idea that the Bible has laid down a blanket prohibition against judging is simply not true.

In fact, it is the exact opposite of what the Bible teaches, and Esther knew that. She looked right over at the king, pointed at Haman, and said, "That man, Haman, is wicked!" Was she doing wrong by judging him? Absolutely not. She was doing right by judging him. Furthermore, she was right in what she judged about him. He was wicked, and he needed to be pointed out as such.

Now, let's get back to Haman. The Bible tells us that when Esther pointed him out like that, he was "afraid before the king and queen." That's good, very good. Wicked people need to be afraid of those in authority. If they aren't, then those in authority are not doing their jobs. Haman, for the first time in this book, was terrified.

A Turn of Poetic Justice

Esther 7:7 *And the king arising from the banquet of wine in his wrath went into the palace garden: and Haman stood up to make request for his life to Esther the queen; for he saw that there was evil determined against him by the king.*

This is the point at which everything finally clicked for the king. He now knew that the people that Haman had decided to kill were the Jews. He now knew that his wife was a Jew. He now knew that Haman had tricked him into passing a law that was going to cost him the wife that he was crazy about. He now knew that Haman, the man he had trusted with everything, was a liar. The realization of all of these things all at once sent him into such a homicidal rage that he had to get up, leave the room for a moment, and get outside to clear his thoughts.

Haman knew he was in deep, deep trouble, and the most amazing thing is, he also had to realize at this point that he had been guilty of a major oversight, one that was likely to cost him his life. That oversight is this: he wrote into law that the Jews were to be destroyed, but he did not write one thing into that law protecting himself! If he had written that he could not be harmed in any way, by anyone, who did not like what had been written or done, then even the king himself could not have touched him.

Realizing that, Haman knew that he had only one choice, and that was the choice that he expected all of the Jews across the world to have: he had the choice to fall on his face and beg for his life. That is all he had! And since Esther was the lovely spider that set all of this elaborate trap for him, luring him before the presence of the king to expose him, she is the one to whom he must beg. The king has already told her three times that she can have whatever she wants. So this wicked man, who has plotted to kill her and all of her entire race, falls on his face before her to beg for mercy. I'm thinking, "NO..."

When Haman fell before the queen, he did not do it gracefully.

Esther 7:8 *Then the king returned out of the palace garden into the place of the banquet of wine; and Haman was **fallen** upon the bed whereon Esther was. Then said the king, Will he force the queen also before me in the house? As the word went out of the king's mouth, they covered Haman's face.*

122

Haman had not gone in a dignified manner to the queen and calmly asked forgiveness and asked to be spared. He is so desperate, so panicky, that he has sprawled out onto her bed... the bed she herself is on. Well now, that doesn't look good, does it! The king certainly didn't think so. He comes back in, angry enough already, and sees Haman sprawled out all over Esther, and he flips his lid! He says basically, "So all he has done isn't bad enough, now he intends to rape my wife with me standing here?!?" And the Bible says that as those words came out of his mouth, they, they being the guards in the room, covered Haman's face. In other words, they put a sack over his head, like they always did even up into the middle ages, with someone that was about to be executed.

I want to give you this thought and then we will come back to it at the end of the chapter: the last sight Haman ever saw was the face of the one whom he had tried to destroy.

Esther 7:9 *And Harbonah, one of the chamberlains, said before the king, Behold also, the gallows fifty cubits high, which Haman had made for Mordecai, who had spoken good for the king, standeth in the house of Haman. Then the king said, Hang him thereon.*

We don't know much about this man, Harbonah, spoken of in this verse. What we do know is that he said very few words, but he made all of them count. He said, "King, this guy just built a gallows 75 feet high in his front yard. He intended to hang Mordecai on it. You know, the same Mordecai that you just honored because he saved your life."

That bit of information was brand new to the king, but there is no way he is going to be shocked by it at this point. He

123

responded with a few simple words, "Hang him (Haman) on it!" You know that is exactly what Harbonah was thinking.

Esther 7:10 *So they hanged Haman on the gallows that he had prepared for Mordecai. Then was the king's wrath pacified.*

By this point in time, Haman had no choice in the matter. He could have done right, but he chose to do wrong, and finally, judgment fell. He was blindfolded with that hood and marched from the palace. He probably recognized the creaking of his own gate as he was marched into his courtyard. Then it was up seven or eight flights of stairs, where moments later, his miserable life abruptly ended.

* * * * *

I want to go back to the thought I gave you a moment ago as we draw this chapter to a close. The last sight that Haman ever saw was the face of the one whom he had tried to destroy. He didn't realize that Esther was who he was fighting against, though. He thought he was fighting against powerless people, never realizing he was fighting against someone in a crown!

This is exactly what it is like for every atheist, agnostic, scoffer, and skeptic. They think they are fighting against a weak, helpless, maybe even a non-existent figure. But one day they are going to fall before him in terror, while angels cover up their face and drag them away. Friend, I would much rather His face be what I see every day for all of eternity, than have His face be the last thing I ever see before I am cast into outer darkness.

But there is one more thing we should know before we leave this chapter. By fighting against the bride, Haman unwittingly found himself fighting against the king. That should give tremendous pause to any who decide to fight against the church, the bride of Christ! If Ahasuerus angrily defended his bride, bought with trinkets, how much more will the God of Heaven angrily defend His bride, bought with His own blood!

Chapter 8
Undoing the Vileness That Outlasts the Villain

Esther 8:1 *On that day did the king Ahasuerus give the house of Haman the Jews' enemy unto Esther the queen. And Mordecai came before the king; for Esther had told what he was unto her. 2 And the king took off his ring, which he had taken from Haman, and gave it unto Mordecai. And Esther set Mordecai over the house of Haman. 3 And Esther spake yet again before the king, and fell down at his feet, and besought him with tears to put away the mischief of Haman the Agagite, and his device that he had devised against the Jews. 4 Then the king held out the golden sceptre toward Esther. So Esther arose, and stood before the king, 5 And said, If it please the king, and if I have found favour in his sight, and the thing seem right before the king, and I be pleasing in his eyes, let it be written to reverse the letters devised by Haman the son of Hammedatha the Agagite, which he wrote to destroy the Jews which are in all the king's provinces: 6 For how can I endure to see the evil that shall come unto my people? or how can I endure to see the destruction of my kindred? 7 Then the king Ahasuerus said unto Esther the queen and to Mordecai the*

Jew, Behold, I have given Esther the house of Haman, and him they have hanged upon the gallows, because he laid his hand upon the Jews. **8** *Write ye also for the Jews, as it liketh you, in the king's name, and seal it with the king's ring: for the writing which is written in the king's name, and sealed with the king's ring, may no man reverse.* **9** *Then were the king's scribes called at that time in the third month, that is, the month Sivan, on the three and twentieth day thereof; and it was written according to all that Mordecai commanded unto the Jews, and to the lieutenants, and the deputies and rulers of the provinces which are from India unto Ethiopia, an hundred twenty and seven provinces, unto every province according to the writing thereof, and unto every people after their language, and to the Jews according to their writing, and according to their language.* **10** *And he wrote in the king Ahasuerus' name, and sealed it with the king's ring, and sent letters by posts on horseback, and riders on mules, camels, and young dromedaries:* **11** *Wherein the king granted the Jews which were in every city to gather themselves together, and to stand for their life, to destroy, to slay, and to cause to perish, all the power of the people and province that would assault them, both little ones and women, and to take the spoil of them for a prey,* **12** *Upon one day in all the provinces of king Ahasuerus, namely, upon the thirteenth day of the twelfth month, which is the month Adar.* **13** *The copy of the writing for a commandment to be given in every province was published unto all people, and that the Jews should be ready against that day to avenge themselves on their enemies.* **14** *So the posts that rode upon mules and camels went out, being hastened and pressed on by the king's commandment. And the decree was* *given at Shushan the palace.* **15** *And Mordecai went out from the presence of the king in royal apparel of blue and white, and with a great crown of gold, and with a garment of fine linen and purple: and the city of Shushan rejoiced and was glad.* **16** *The Jews had light, and gladness, and joy, and honour.* **17** *And in every province, and in every city, whithersoever the king's commandment and his decree came, the Jews had joy and gladness, a feast and a good day. And many of the people of the land became Jews; for the fear of the Jews fell upon them.*

If evil had a shelf life equal to that of its founder, the world would be a much better, much safer place. Unfortunately, evil, once given birth, tends to outlive its founder. Muhammad founded his evil in the seventh century, and buildings are still falling because of it in the twenty-first century. Darwin started his evil generations ago, and it has lived far beyond him. Marx and Engels, Westcott and Hort, the wrong things that people establish far outlive them and impact generations to come.

Haman was dead. He hung on his own gallows at the end of chapter seven. Yet the evil that he set in motion was still alive and well and was only going to get worse if not somehow stopped. Many people are in the same condition today as the Jews were then. Someone has unleashed an evil against them and even after that person is no longer around the evil he or she birthed is still doing damage. Many a person was abused or molested as a child and even after the villain is gone or dead there are still things crumbling in that person's life. Many people have lost a loved one due to a drunk driver and even if the drunk driver himself died as well it doesn't bring back the one they lost. Many pastors have had people tell vicious lies about them and their church and even after the liar is dead and in the grave the lie lives on, stronger than ever. Many countries have endured brutal dictatorships and even after the dictator has been rightly destroyed the damage he did goes on for years.

I want to examine in this chapter how Mordecai and Esther dealt with the effects of Haman's decree.

An Unrealized Power

Esther 8:1 *On that day did the king Ahasuerus give the house of Haman the Jews' enemy unto Esther the queen. And Mordecai came before the king; for Esther had told what he was unto her. 2 And the king took off his ring, which he had taken from Haman, and gave it unto Mordecai. And Esther set Mordecai over the house of Haman.*

When Haman did what he did, it was an assault against Esther, whether he realized it or not. So when Haman was killed, all of the possessions of Haman (including all of his family) were given to Esther. These people were every bit as wicked and evil as Haman, the head of the home. It was Haman's wife that suggested the gallows be built for Mordecai. Haman was now dead, and as a partial payment for the wrong that he had done to Esther and her people, the house of Haman was given to her.

And then there was the matter of the ring. Back in chapter three the king had taken off his royal signet ring and given it to Haman. Haman was allowed to use that ring to sign the evil law that would destroy the Jews. When he pressed that ring into the blob of wax sealing that decree, it was as powerful as if Ahasuerus himself had done it. But when the law was signed, the king apparently did not even bother to ask for his ring back! His trust in Haman was so complete that he just let him keep on wearing the ring. That is positively amazing. There is no imagining just how much damage he could have caused in a very short time with that much power literally at his fingertips!

With Haman being carried away to the gallows, the king took his ring back off of Haman's soon to be cold dead hands. Then just a few minutes later, he gave it away yet again. The text tells us that Esther told the king who Mordecai was to her, and the king then gave that ring to Mordecai. Several things leap out to me in considering those words.

I am first of all amazed by the humility and restraint of Mordecai. Esther has been queen for four or five years now. All of that time, Mordecai said nothing about being related to her. He never tried to gain from her glory. He let her shine, and he was content to stay in the shadows. Even when Haman was trying to hang him, he never tried to get Esther to use her position to do him any personal favors. This was an amazing man.

I am also amazed by the fact that God brought so many things together all at once. Please, remember that when dealing with the Persian Empire, we are dealing with 100 million people or so. Out of all of those people, out of all of those years, how unlikely is it to see this series of events:

Queen Vashti gets divorced. A beauty pageant takes place. Out of 100 million people, a girl right there in Shushan ends up as the new queen. Her adoptive father is an old man named Mordecai, but no one knows that. Mordecai just happens to overhear a plot against the king's life and tells it to Esther, who just happens to be the new queen. The king's life is saved, but he just happens to forget what Mordecai did for him. Later, the king's most trusted advisor, out of a kingdom of 100 million people, just happens to get furiously angry at that one old man named Mordecai. He decides to kill Mordecai and all of the Jews. Mordecai gets word to Esther. Esther goes before the king and does her little mystery game. That night, the king just happens to not be able to sleep. He just happens to call for someone to read him the Chronicles of the Kings of Persia. The reader just happens to read about the time Mordecai saved the king's life. The king just happens to realize that no honor was done to Mordecai for this. The king then just happens to ask who is in the court, and it just so happens that at that weird hour of the night, Haman is out there. He is there to ask the king for permission to hang Mordecai, whom the king just happened to finish reading about at that exact moment. The king calls Haman in and asks him what should be done to a man that the king wants to honor. Haman just happens to think he himself is that man. A moment later, Haman just happens to find himself preparing a processional to honor Mordecai, the man he was there to try to hang. Then it just so happens that Haman gets called to the banquet at which time Esther points him out as the man trying to kill her and her people. The king, enraged, kills Haman. Then, to top it off, the king finds out that the man he just honored for saving his life is, in fact, the man that raised his wife, Esther, like a daughter!

If King Ahasuerus didn't get saved after all of this, he is the biggest fool to ever walk the face of the planet. All of those "just so happens" really didn't "just so happen." God had His hand in every step of the process. He was working behind the scene to put all of the pieces in the exact right place at the exact right time.

After the king gave Esther the house of Haman, Esther turned around and gave it to Mordecai.

Esther 8:3 *And Esther spake yet again before the king, and fell down at his feet, and besought him with tears to put away the mischief of Haman the Agagite, and his device that he had devised against the Jews.*

Esther knew that even though the villain was gone, the decree was still in effect. No one was going to touch her at that point, no one was going to touch Mordecai at that point, but millions of others would not be so fortunate. Esther knew better than to be complacent and satisfied in her own safety. She begged the king to find some way to spare the lives of millions of people that she did not even know. That is an excellent picture of how we who have been saved should feel about the lost of this world, people who will go to Hell unless we reach them with the gospel.

Esther 8:4 *Then the king held out the golden sceptre toward Esther. So Esther arose, and stood before the king,* **5** *And said, If it please the king, and if I have found favour in his sight, and the thing seem right before the king, and I be pleasing in his eyes, let it be written to reverse the letters devised by Haman the son of Hammedatha the Agagite, which he wrote to destroy the Jews which are in all the king's provinces:* **6** *For how can I endure to see the evil that shall come unto my people? or how can I endure to see the destruction of my kindred?*

For the second time, the king extended the scepter out to Esther. Esther rose from off of the ground, where she had been wetting the ground with her tears and stood before him. Can you imagine that beautiful girl, with tears streaking her lovely face, in anguish of heart for millions who were about to perish? This girl was broken. She said, "How can I endure to see the evil that shall come unto my people? or how can I endure to see the destruction of my kindred?" She genuinely cared for others, people she had not even met. This was a remarkable woman; she will be a joy to speak to in eternity I think.

Esther asked the king to reverse the letters that Haman had written. The problem was, it could not be done. The law of the Medes and Persians could not be altered. But what could be altered were the effects of that law.

Esther 8:7 *Then the king Ahasuerus said unto Esther the queen and to Mordecai the Jew, Behold, I have given Esther the house of Haman, and him they have hanged upon the gallows, because he laid his hand upon the Jews. 8 Write ye also for the Jews, as it liketh you, in the king's name, and seal it with the king's ring: for the writing which is written in the king's name, and sealed with the king's ring, may no man reverse.*

Ahasuerus was dumb enough to trust Haman with his ring and smart enough to trust Mordecai with it. He knew that the previous writing could not be undone, but he also knew that Mordecai was shrewd enough to figure out a way to write something new that would blunt the effects of that previous law.

This was a power that Esther did not seem to fully realize, or she would not have still been crying! Whoever held the ring held the power. She and Mordecai held the ring! They held the king's signet. His power was their power.

I believe that children of God today are much like broken-hearted, tear-soaked Esther. We don't seem to realize what we were given the day the King took us into His favor:

James 1:5 *If any of you lack wisdom, let him ask of God, that giveth to all men liberally, and upbraideth not; and it shall be given him.*

Philippians 4:13 *I can do all things through Christ which strengtheneth me.*

James 5:16b *...The effectual fervent prayer of a righteous man availeth much.*

Psalm 84:11 *For the LORD God is a sun and shield: the LORD will give grace and glory: no good thing will he withhold from them that walk uprightly.*

Hebrews 13:5b *I will never leave thee, nor forsake thee.*

1 John 4:4 *Ye are of God, little children, and have overcome them: because greater is he that is in you, than he that is in the world.*

The power at our disposal is incredible, even more so than what Mordecai had. Mordecai was wearing the king's ring; we are wearing the King's blood! Hold your head up high, Child of God; you have an unrealized power that you can tap into every time you go before God in prayer.

An Urgent Publishing

Esther 8:9 *Then were the king's scribes called at that time in the third month, that is, the month Sivan, on the three and twentieth day thereof; and it was written according to all that Mordecai commanded unto the Jews, and to the lieutenants, and the deputies and rulers of the provinces which are from India unto Ethiopia, an hundred twenty and seven provinces, unto every province according to the writing thereof, and unto every people after their language, and to the Jews according to their writing, and according to their language.*

When the writing was prepared and finalized, nine months remained until the day of the Jews attempted extermination. Mordecai had gone to work and written a new law designed to prevent that extermination from happening. Like the first decree, it would have to be gotten into every corner of the empire, 127 provinces, translated into multiple languages. This was no small task.

Esther 8:10 *And he wrote in the king Ahasuerus' name, and sealed it with the king's ring, and sent letters by posts on horseback, and riders on mules, camels, and young dromedaries:*

When the first decree was sent out, the Bible simply says that it was sent by posts (Esther 3:13). In Esther 8:10, it says the new decree was sent by posts on horseback, mules, camels, and dromedaries. These were four different types of animals. The implication seems to be that they were using whatever they had at their disposal. The first decree would have gotten the choicest of animals available to send out the word. They would not be back yet, in fact, some of them would still be traveling to get to their destination. This second set of animals and riders was literally going to be in hot pursuit of the first set. Can you imagine that scene, as the riders are mounting up waiting for the command to leave? I can see them tightening the cinches, securing their packs, mounting up. I can see Mordecai and Esther walking down the line, touching each animal on the neck. I can see Esther whispering in the ear of a young horse, "Fly like the wind; the lives of my people depend on it." When the command was given, I can just imagine a cloud of dust rising across the desert sands, as each rider drove his beast hard, desperate to reach his destination in time.

When a message is that important, you do whatever you have to do to get it out. This is the same way we should be treating the Gospel message. If you have to get the message out by Chevy, do it. If you have to get it out by Moped, do it. If you have to get it out by paddle boat, do it. If you have to get it out on foot, do it. If you have to fly across the sea to carry the message, do it. We are carrying the most important message in the history of mankind, so mount up and ride!

Esther 8:11 *Wherein the king granted the Jews which were in every city to gather themselves together, and to stand for their life, to destroy, to slay, and to cause to perish, all the power of the people and province that would assault them, both little ones and women, and to take the spoil of them for a prey,* **12** *Upon one day in all the provinces of king Ahasuerus, namely, upon the thirteenth day of the twelfth month, which is the month Adar.* **13** *The copy of the writing for a commandment to be given in every province was published* *unto all people, and that the Jews should be ready against that day to avenge themselves on their enemies.*

These verses give us the content of the writing of Mordecai. It was a decree of self defense. The Jews were commanded to "stand for their lives." They were told to gather together and fight back.

Never think for a moment that the Bible encourages pacifism. It does not. The Quakers and the Amish are simply wrong. The Bible encourages self defense, over and over again. If you won't stand, you are not a man. David stood and fought against Goliath. The entire book of numbers was about God raising an army in which all males age twenty and up were expected to participate. God called Himself "A Man of War." The Bible never encourages pacifism!

Are we to fight for every little slap in the face or every insult? No. We can afford to turn the other cheek on those. But when it comes time to either fight or be killed, we better be ready to fight. When it comes time to fire the gun or see our wives and kids assaulted, we better fire the gun. When it comes time to go to war or have our country destroyed, we better go to war. The Jews were about to be slaughtered, and the solution was for them to gather themselves together and fight back.

An interesting part of the decree was also that they were allowed to take the possessions of their dead enemies as spoils of war. Try and remember that because in the next chapter we will see it again in a rather unique light.

Esther 8:14 *So the posts that rode upon mules and camels went out, being hastened and pressed on by the king's* *commandment. And the decree was given at Shushan the palace.*

The riders went, and they went quickly. They were "hastened and pressed on by the king's commandment." It was now known that the queen was one of these Jews, the people that were to be destroyed. Slow down on that ride and you would face the wrath of a very angry king Ahasuerus.

At the end of verse fourteen a note is added. The decree was given at Shushan the palace. The former decree had also been given there. A man had stood up and loudly read the decree that the Jews must be killed. Now either that same man, or maybe another, stands up in that exact same place and loudly reads that the Jews are commanded to stand together and fight for their lives. What has just happened is that a showdown has been set up– nine months away.

Those would have to be nine very interesting months. Day after day Jews and non Jews would rub shoulders, do business together, eat together, warily eyeing one another. Day after day people would wonder who would try to kill in a few months, and who would try and stay out of it. People would smile at each other, hug, and all the while be looking for a good place to stick the knife when the day of the dice finally came.

Regardless, an urgent publishing had been sent out as a means of undoing the vileness that outlasts the villain.

An Uncomfortable People

Esther 8:15 *And Mordecai went out from the presence of the king in royal apparel of blue and white, and with a great crown of gold, and with a garment of fine linen and* *purple: and the city of Shushan rejoiced and was glad.* **16** *The Jews had light, and gladness, and joy, and honour.* **17** *And in every province, and in every city, whithersoever the king's commandment and his decree came, the Jews had joy and gladness, a feast and a good day. And many of the people of the land became Jews; for the fear of the Jews fell upon them.*

Hours earlier Mordecai had been given a set of royal clothes and a royal crown on a temporary basis. But now, once it was revealed who he was and what a value he had been to the king, he was given those clothes and crown on a permanent basis. He became a living illustration of the child of God. When we arrive before the King and it is revealed who we really are, joint heirs with Christ, we will be arrayed in royal garments permanently. Any honor we get here is only temporary, but the honors we will receive in Heaven are permanent.

Verse sixteen tells us that the Jews had light and gladness and joy and honor. These phrases let us know that the dark storm clouds had rolled away, and the tears had been replaced by smiles. Were there no more battles to fight? There were. In fact, their biggest battle lay before them. They would literally find themselves in a fight for their very lives, and they knew it. This is also an excellent illustration of the Christian life. When we get saved, we will be happy and joyful, but we need to be happy and joyful while still realizing that our greatest battles still lay ahead of us!

Verse seventeen tells us that the Jews everywhere had joy, gladness, a feast, and a good day. I have heard people blast the idea of God's people having fellowship meals together, saying that they are somehow unspiritual. I have been in the agonizingly depressing company of those that believed that we should always be grim and hard and that any smiling or laughing or rejoicing will surely send people to Hell. Those people are unbiblical, unstable, and unable to sustain themselves under the constant pressure that they place upon themselves. The Jews knew that a celebration was in order and so they celebrated.

But we should lastly note from verse seventeen that "many of the people of the land became Jews; for the fear of the Jews fell upon them." The people of the Persian Empire became very uncomfortable being on the other side of the battle lines against the Jews. The Jews became scary to them because they suddenly had enormous strength and power. Esther was the queen. Mordecai was the second in command of the kingdom. Their strength made people uncomfortable and turned many of their enemies into allies.

On a practical level, this is something America should learn from. We have enemies all about and a present administration that seems determined to try to make friends out of them by making our country weak. The idea seems to be that if we just gut our military, stop using real bullets, and turn our soldiers into humanitarians we will have fewer enemies. No, we will have far MORE enemies if we do that.

On a spiritual level, I am interested in seeing God's people be both godly enough and also wise enough to become very strong. Strength tends to turn enemies into friends. Strength tends to help undo the vileness that outlasts the villain.

Chapter 9

The Day of the Dice

Esther 9:1 *Now in the twelfth month, that is, the month Adar, on the thirteenth day of the same, when the king's commandment and his decree drew near to be put in execution, in the day that the enemies of the Jews hoped to have power over them, (though it was turned to the contrary, that the Jews had rule over them that hated them;)* **2** *The Jews gathered themselves together in their cities throughout all the provinces of the king Ahasuerus, to lay hand on such as sought their hurt: and no man could withstand them; for the fear of them fell upon all people.* **3** *And all the rulers of the provinces, and the lieutenants, and the deputies, and officers of the king, helped the Jews; because the fear of Mordecai fell upon them.* **4** *For Mordecai was great in the king's house, and his fame went out throughout all the provinces: for this man Mordecai waxed greater and greater.* **5** *Thus the Jews smote all their enemies with the stroke of the sword, and slaughter, and destruction, and did what they would unto those that hated them.* **6** *And in Shushan the palace the Jews slew and destroyed five hundred men.* **7** *And Parshandatha, and Dalphon, and Aspatha,* **8** *And Poratha, and Adalia, and Aridatha,* **9** *And Parmashta, and Arisai, and Aridai, and*

Vajezatha, **10** *The ten sons of Haman the son of Hammedatha, the enemy of the Jews, slew they; but on the spoil laid they not their hand.* **11** *On that day the number of those that were slain in Shushan the palace was brought before the king.* **12** *And the king said unto Esther the queen, The Jews have slain and destroyed five hundred men in Shushan the palace, and the ten sons of Haman; what have they done in the rest of the king's provinces? now what is thy petition? and it shall be granted thee: or what is thy request further? and it shall be done.* **13** *Then said Esther, If it please the king, let it be granted to the Jews which are in Shushan to do to morrow also according unto this day's decree, and let Haman's ten sons be hanged upon the gallows.* **14** *And the king commanded it so to be done: and the decree was given at Shushan; and they hanged Haman's ten sons.* **15** *For the Jews that were in Shushan gathered themselves together on the fourteenth day also of the month Adar, and slew three hundred men at Shushan; but on the prey they laid not their hand.* **16** *But the other Jews that were in the king's provinces gathered themselves together, and stood for their lives, and had rest from their enemies, and slew of their foes seventy and five thousand, but they laid not their hands on the prey,* **17** *On the thirteenth day of the month Adar; and on the fourteenth day of the same rested they, and made it a day of feasting and gladness.* **18** *But the Jews that were at Shushan assembled together on the thirteenth day thereof, and on the fourteenth thereof; and on the fifteenth day of the same they rested, and made it a day of feasting and gladness.* **19** *Therefore the Jews of the villages, that dwelt in the unwalled towns, made the fourteenth day of the month Adar a day of gladness and feasting, and a good day, and of* *sending portions one to another.* **20** *And Mordecai wrote these things, and sent letters unto all the Jews that were in all the provinces of the king Ahasuerus, both nigh and far,* **21** *To stablish this among them, that they should keep the fourteenth day of the month Adar, and the fifteenth day of the same, yearly,* **22** *As the days wherein the Jews rested from their enemies, and the month which was turned unto them from sorrow to joy, and from mourning into a good day: that they should make them days of feasting and joy, and of sending portions one to another, and gifts to the poor.* **23** *And the Jews undertook to do as they had begun, and as Mordecai had written unto them;* **24** *Because Haman the son of Hammedatha, the Agagite, the enemy of all the Jews, had devised against the Jews to destroy them, and had cast Pur, that is, the lot, to consume them, and to destroy them;* **25** *But when Esther came before the king, he commanded by letters that his wicked device, which he devised against the Jews, should return upon his own head, and that he and his sons should be hanged on the gallows.* **26** *Wherefore they called these days Purim after the name of Pur. Therefore for all the words of this letter, and of that which they had seen concerning this matter, and which had come unto them,* **27** *The Jews ordained, and took upon them, and upon their seed, and upon all such as joined themselves unto them, so as it should not fail, that they would keep these two days according to their writing, and according to their appointed time every year;* **28** *And that these days should be remembered and kept throughout every generation, every family, every province, and every city; and that these days of Purim should not fail from among the Jews, nor the memorial of them perish from*

145

their seed. **29** *Then Esther the queen, the daughter of Abihail, and Mordecai the Jew, wrote with all authority, to confirm this second letter of Purim.* **30** *And he sent the letters unto all the Jews, to the hundred twenty and seven provinces of the kingdom of Ahasuerus, with words of peace and truth,* **31** *To confirm these days of Purim in their times appointed, according as Mordecai the Jew and Esther the queen had enjoined them, and as they had decreed for themselves and for their seed, the matters of the fastings and their cry.* **32** *And the decree of Esther confirmed these matters of Purim; and it was written in the book.*

Esther 10:1 *And the king Ahasuerus laid a tribute upon the land, and upon the isles of the sea.* **2** *And all the acts of his power and of his might, and the declaration of the greatness of Mordecai, whereunto the king advanced him, are they not written in the book of the chronicles of the kings of Media and Persia?* **3** *For Mordecai the Jew was next unto king Ahasuerus, and great among the Jews, and accepted of the multitude of his brethren, seeking the wealth of his people, and speaking peace to all his seed.*

There are things that often appear on our calendars, significant things, which people are nearly oblivious to. One of those things occurs in our February or March each year. It is the Jewish feast of Purim. It is what I call *The Day of the Dice.* It is the day that wicked Haman chose by the casting of lots to destroy the Jews. It became the day that the Jews not only survived but actually prevailed against their enemies. That is the subject matter of Esther chapters nine and ten.

A Standing Together

Esther 9:1 *Now in the twelfth month, that is, the month Adar, on the thirteenth day of the same, when the king's commandment and his decree drew near to be put in execution, in the day that the enemies of the Jews hoped to have power over them, (though it was turned to the contrary, that the Jews had rule over them that hated them;)*

As the text begins to tell us of the events of the day of Purim, it draws our attention to the fact that God's people, the Jews, were hated. It is always going to be like this. Whomever God loves, the world will hate. The Jews have experienced this for a very long time in country after country around the world. This is what convinced them of the need to have their own country again. No matter what country they were in, they always became scapegoats.

Christians through the years have experienced a great deal of this treatment as well. And I don't just mean in Muslim countries around the world, I mean even right here in supposedly Christian America.

In December of 1998, Alan Dershowitz had this to say: "Jerry Falwell and the Christian right are evil; they are absolutely demonic."

Also in December of 1998, this bit of liberal tolerance was thrown out there by that paragon of kindness, Alec Baldwin: "If we lived in another country, do you know what we would do? We would stone (Christian senator) Henry Hyde and his wife and kids to death!"

A few years ago homosexual activists surrounded a church in California and started shouting, "Bring back the lions! Bring back the lions!"

Should we be surprised by this? No, because Jesus said:

John 15:18 *If the world hate you, ye know that it hated me before it hated you.* **19** *If ye were of the world, the world would love his own: but because ye are not of the world, but I have chosen you out of the world, therefore the world hateth you.* **20** *Remember the word that I said unto you, The servant is not greater than his lord. If they have persecuted me, they will also persecute you; if they have kept my saying, they will keep yours also.*

The Jews knew enough to expect it, and we should as well.

Esther 9:2 *The Jews gathered themselves together in their cities throughout all the provinces of the king Ahasuerus, to lay hand on such as sought their hurt: and no man could withstand them; for the fear of them fell upon all people.*

Faced with destruction, the Jews "gathered themselves together." They understood that individually they stood very little chance of surviving, but together they stood a very good chance of surviving. This is something Christians and churches today seem to very rarely understand.

Let me tell you what the world usually sees when they look at churches. They see pastors that use churches as stepping stones for bigger and bigger ministries. They see pastors who bolt for greener pastures every time there is trouble. They see pastors who view the pastorate as a job rather than a calling. These pastors are hirelings, and as a result, the sheep end up scattered.

But then there is the pew. In the pew, they see people who, as regular as the New Year, either split or splinter. They see churches started all over town in little storefront buildings

148

with a bunch of people that didn't get their way where they were going to church, so they all left and started a new one. The lost world sees splits named Unity, angry splinter groups named Friendship, and the same old same old named New Start, and we wonder why the church has no credibility.

The world sees this. They see what I call "Christians Behaving Badly," and they want nothing to do with God as a result. And what is the result to the church? The church becomes so weak that they have no strength to stand against the attacks the devil levels against them. Churches better get into the habit of members getting along with other members and members getting along with pastor.

Churches also better get into the habit of getting along with other Bible believing churches! It is a sad state of affairs in our land when Bible believing, right doctrine holding, properly behaving churches view each other as enemies.

This applies to a nation as well, and in the case of America, it does so in a frightening manner. Our country once had a unity of belief and purpose. But years of indoctrination have produced a belief in the doctrine of multi-culturalism. This has accomplished the enemy's task of weakening our country far more effectively than their bombs or bullets could ever do. We are not stronger by being a hodge-podge of different beliefs and purposes. We are stronger when all genders, races, creeds, and backgrounds are willingly subservient to the principles upon which this country was founded. Unity breeds strength, division into disparate groups breeds weakness.

Esther 9:3 *And all the rulers of the provinces, and the lieutenants, and the deputies, and officers of the king, helped*

149

the Jews; because the fear of Mordecai fell upon them. **4** *For Mordecai was great in the king's house, and his fame went out throughout all the provinces: for this man Mordecai waxed greater and greater.*

At the beginning of his story Mordecai seemed destined to fail. He was old, powerless, and stubborn about right and wrong. He refused to make things easier on himself by going along to get along. He could have bowed before Haman like everyone else and had a comfortable life of groveling. But Mordecai knew that standing for right was worth doing even if it meant he would lose everything. By the end of his story, he was the second in command of the empire. Mordecai was the second Jew to have this as his story. He doubtless made his multi-great uncle Joseph proud as he looked down from Heaven!

Esther 9:5 *Thus the Jews smote all their enemies with the stroke of the sword, and slaughter, and destruction, and did what they would unto those that hated them.* **6** *And in Shushan the palace the Jews slew and destroyed five hundred men.* **7** *And Parshandatha, and Dalphon, and Aspatha,* **8** *And Poratha, and Adalia, and Aridatha,* **9** *And Parmashta, and Arisai, and Aridai, and Vajezatha,* **10a** *The ten sons of Haman the son of Hammedatha, the enemy of the Jews, slew they;*

When the day of the dice came, when the battle was joined, it was a rout. The Jews slaughtered their enemies. In this verse we are specifically told of two groups. We are first informed that there were five hundred people killed in Shushan the Palace. This is stunning, almost incomprehensible. It was very well known by this point how the king felt on this matter. It was very well known that Queen

Esther was a Jew and that Mordecai was as well. Yet in the face of all of that, there were still five hundred people willing to try and destroy the Jews there in the palace! Never underestimate Satan's hatred of the Jewish people and his ability to whip the world into an anti-Semitic frenzy.

We are also informed that the ten sons of Haman were killed. Their names were given to us in verses seven and eight. Haman had lived long enough to produce ten children, and they had obviously lived long enough to become just like their father. Dads, be careful what you do and how you teach your children. If the path you are walking on leads to destruction, you can probably also hear little footsteps walking behind you.

A Spoil Untouched

Esther 9:10b *... but on the spoil laid they not their hand.*

For now, just file this thought away. They destroyed their enemies, yet they did not touch or take any of their possessions.

Esther 9:11 *On that day the number of those that were slain in Shushan the palace was brought before the king.* **12** *And the king said unto Esther the queen, The Jews have slain and destroyed five hundred men in Shushan the palace, and the ten sons of Haman; what have they done in the rest of the king's provinces? now what is thy petition? and it shall be granted thee: or what is thy request further? and it shall be done.* **13** *Then said Esther, If it please the king, let it be granted to the Jews which are in Shushan to do to morrow also according unto this day's decree, and let Haman's ten sons be hanged upon the gallows.* **14** *And the king commanded* *it so to be done: and the decree was given at Shushan; and they hanged Haman's ten sons.* **15a** *For the Jews that were in Shushan gathered themselves together on the fourteenth day also of the month Adar, and slew three hundred men at Shushan;*

In verse twelve we find just how actively involved Esther was with all that happened. This was no shrinking violet; the king actually asked *her* for the body count from the rest of the 127 provinces! He then proceeded to ask her what else she would like for him to do for her. Her answer was extremely wise. She first of all requested that the ten sons of Haman that had already been killed in the fighting have their dead bodies publically hanged. The reason for this was to serve as a warning not to mess with the Jews. That kind of thing tends to draw attention and serve as something of a deterrent. The second thing she requested was that the Jews be allowed to defend themselves on the next day as well. She knew that just because the referee rings the bell, it does not necessarily mean that an opponent will not hit you late. She was making preparations in advance rather than relying on reactions after the fact.

And she was right. On the fourteenth, the day after the decree had expired, another battle or series of battles broke out right there in the palace. The enemies of the Jews did not care that their day of destruction had ended yesterday; they arbitrarily extended it another day. They were just like modern day Muslims who think nothing about bombing Jews on the Sabbath or on a Jewish Holiday, or bombing Christians on Christmas or Easter, or of violating every cease fire and treaty they have ever agreed to. But the preparations of Esther did the job. Knowing that they could defend themselves yet again, day two resulted in 300 more enemies dead there in the palace.

Esther 9:15b *... but on the prey they laid not their hand.*

This is the second time in this chapter it has been observed that they did not touch any of the spoils of this war. File this one away as well; we will come back to this thought shortly.

Esther 9:16 *But the other Jews that were in the king's provinces gathered themselves together, and stood for their lives, and had rest from their enemies, and slew of their foes seventy and five thousand, but they laid not their hands on the prey,*

This is now the third time it has been observed that they did not take anything from those they had beaten and killed. This is all the more interesting in light of the words written in the decree of Esther and Mordecai:

Esther 8:11 *Wherein the king granted the Jews which were in every city to gather themselves together, and to stand for their life, to destroy, to slay, and to cause to perish, all the power of the people and province that would assault them, both little ones and women, and to take the spoil of them for a prey,*

The decree specifically allowed them to take the possessions of those that they killed in battle. But all across the empire, they refused to do so. Just because something is *allowed* does not mean that it is *wise*. These Jews, I do not know if they somehow coordinated or if they just all understood it, did the wise thing rather than the allowed thing. If they had taken the spoils, what would people have said of them? "Those typical greedy Jews! No wonder Haman wanted to destroy them, all they are interested in is taking what is not theirs, and they will even kill to do it!" Would it have been true? No. But would people have believed it anyway? Yes. They knew that. And a prominent person in their past had taught them what was truly important.

Proverbs 22:1 *A good name is rather to be chosen than great riches, and loving favour rather than silver and gold.*

They were guarding their testimony. People are going to accuse; it is what people do. We need to live our lives as carefully as possible to make our accusers look foolish. This is one reason why my wife is also the church secretary, other than the fact that she is really good at it. By me being with her all day every day, anyone that ever tries to accuse me of being a womanizer is going to look like the moron they actually are to anyone that knows us!

A Sending of Gifts

Esther 9:17 *On the thirteenth day of the month Adar; and on the fourteenth day of the same rested they, and made it a day of feasting and gladness.* **18** *But the Jews that were at Shushan assembled together on the thirteenth day thereof, and on the fourteenth thereof; and on the fifteenth day of the same they rested, and made it a day of feasting and gladness.* **19** *Therefore the Jews of the villages, that dwelt in the unwalled towns, made the fourteenth day of the month Adar a day of gladness and feasting, and a good day, and of sending portions one to another.*

As has been previously noted, there was a bit of a difference between the events in Shushan and the rest of the

154

empire. In Shushan there were two days of fighting, the thirteenth and fourteenth, and then they rested on the fifteenth. In the rest of the empire there was one day of fighting, the thirteenth, and they rested on the fourteenth.

These two days became a very special holiday to the Jews. The fourteenth day, especially, was singled out as a day of gladness and feasting. On that day, they sent portions, gifts, to each other. The princes and people of the East not only invite their friends to feasts, but it is their custom to send a portion of the banquet to those who cannot well come to it, especially their relations and those who are detained at home in a state of sorrow or distress.[19] In other words, the Jews, rich and poor, who had been targeted together, determined that rich and poor should also celebrate together. They sent each other gifts, food, and help; and the entire race of people celebrated what God had done for them. This is an excellent precursor to the wonderful day that we now call Christmas when we do much the same.

Esther 9:20 *And Mordecai wrote these things, and sent letters unto all the Jews that were in all the provinces of the king Ahasuerus, both nigh and far,* **21** *To stablish this among them, that they should keep the fourteenth day of the month Adar, and the fifteenth day of the same, yearly,* **22** *As the days wherein the Jews rested from their enemies, and the month which was turned unto them from sorrow to joy, and from mourning into a good day: that they should make them days of feasting and joy, and of sending portions one to another, and gifts to the poor.*

The feast of Purim became an official Jewish holiday at the authority of Mordecai. He wrote the decree; he sent it out;

he established it. This great and godly man understood what many merely religious men do not understand today: proper celebrations are a gift of God. The world is a hard, brutal place. Job said:

Job 14:1 *Man that is born of a woman is of few days, and full of trouble.*

Since this is true, it is entirely appropriate for us to celebrate those days that are *not* full of trouble! Make the Christmas tree a big one and decorate it lavishly. Buy new dresses and suits for Easter. Send incredible gifts for birthdays, especially mine. Cry and bring flowers on Mother's Day. Send your spouse a Valentine's Day card with those "special coupons" in it. If you want to stand with the anti-holiday, doom and gloom, Scrooge and company crowd, help yourself. I stand with Esther, Mordecai, and Hallmark...

Esther 9:23 *And the Jews undertook to do as they had begun, and as Mordecai had written unto them;* **24** *Because Haman the son of Hammedatha, the Agagite, the enemy of all the Jews, had devised against the Jews to destroy them, and had cast Pur, that is, the lot, to consume them, and to destroy them;* **25** *But when Esther came before the king, he commanded by letters that his wicked device, which he devised against the Jews, should return upon his own head, and that he and his sons should be hanged on the gallows.* **26** *Wherefore they called these days Purim after the name of Pur. Therefore for all the words of this letter, and of that which they had seen concerning this matter, and which had come unto them,* **27** *The Jews ordained, and took upon them, and upon their seed, and upon all such as joined themselves unto them, so as it should not fail, that they would keep these two*

156

days according to their writing, and according to their appointed time every year; 28 And that these days should be remembered and kept throughout every generation, every family, every province, and every city; and that these days of Purim should not fail from among the Jews, nor the memorial of them perish from their seed. 29 Then Esther the queen, the daughter of Abihail, and Mordecai the Jew, wrote with all authority, to confirm this second letter of Purim. 30 And he sent the letters unto all the Jews, to the hundred twenty and seven provinces of the kingdom of Ahasuerus, with words of peace and truth, 31 To confirm these days of Purim in their times appointed, according as Mordecai the Jew and Esther the queen had enjoined them, and as they had decreed for themselves and for their seed, the matters of the fastings and their cry. 32 And the decree of Esther confirmed these matters of Purim; and it was written in the book.

All of these verses deal with the same subject, the institution of the feast of Purim. Verses twenty-four and twenty-five give a two verse summary of what happened, and the rest of the verses deal with the fact that this feast was to be kept by every Jew, forever. Verse twenty-eight adds a very important impetus: they did not ever want their descendants to forget what had happened. A common memory of the past is essential to the survival of a people. That is what makes the current destroyers of American history such enemies. The vast preponderance of public school history books no longer contain the necessary history of America: things like the Constitution, the Declaration of Independence, the founding fathers, the Revolutionary War, the religious underpinnings that motivated our laws, and the like. But public school textbooks will give children a heavy dose of pop culture, socialistic thought, multi-cultural pablum, and things that do nothing to unite us. One of the reasons that the Jews have survived as a people through multiple captivities, multiple dispersions, multiple attempts at annihilation, and thousands of years without a homeland is the fact that they have maintained common holidays and a common history.

America may not be so fortunate. If things continue as they are going, Christmas, Easter, Thanksgiving, and the Fourth of July will either be outlawed or so altered as to be unrecognizable.

A Seeking and Speaking

Esther 10:1 *And the king Ahasuerus laid a tribute upon the land, and upon the isles of the sea.*

In the very first chapter of the book we observed that Ahasuerus was engaged in near constant battles. The Persian Empire would one day fall to the Greeks, though he could not have known this. He did everything in his power to maintain the might of the empire, including taxing it heavily. History obviously tells us that this approach did not keep them from ruin. The evidence shows the contrary, it hastened their ruin, as it does any nation that tries it.

Esther 10:2 *And all the acts of his power and of his might, and the declaration of the greatness of Mordecai, whereunto the king advanced him, are they not written in the book of the chronicles of the kings of Media and Persia?*

Mordecai was a Jew. This Jew was written about in glowing terms in the book of the *Chronicles of the Kings of Media and Persia.* When we consider what name that Persia

158

goes by now, this becomes all the more striking. Ancient Persia became modern day Iran, the most antagonistic nation on Earth toward the Jews. They, like most people, easily forget those to whom they owe a great debt of gratitude.

Esther 10:3 *For Mordecai the Jew was next unto king Ahasuerus, and great among the Jews, and accepted of the multitude of his brethren, seeking the wealth of his people, and speaking peace to all his seed.*

The last phrase of the book, a descriptive phrase about Mordecai, tells us so much about this man:

...seeking the wealth of his people, and speaking peace to all his seed.

Mordecai never seems to have been interested in seeking wealth for himself, but he was interested in seeking it for his people. He never seems to have been concerned with having a peaceful life himself, but he was concerned that his people be at peace. This man was humble, focused on others, resolute, and a person of integrity. Little wonder that he raised a child just like him.

Epilogue

What would a Biblical detective find if he did a forensic analysis of the book of Esther? He would find the fingerprints of God on every page, every chapter, and every line. God was in control even when He could not be seen, heard, or felt. He moved silently across every event of the book, placing people right where they needed to be, right when they needed to be there. He caused sleepless nights at just the right moment. He moved through an empire of 100 million people, and put one special girl in front of the king at the exact moment she needed to be there. When you want to assure yourself that God will be in control when He returns, you will want to read the book of the Revelation. But if you need the calm assurance that He is already in control right now, you will never do better than the book of Esther.

NOTES

[1] Robert Jamieson, A. R. Fausset, David Brown, *A Commentary on the Old and New Testaments*, vol. 2, *Joshua-Esther*, (Peabody, MA:Hendrickson Publishers, 2008), 633.

[2] C. F. Keil, D.D., F. Delitzsch, D.D., *Biblical Commentary on the Old Testament, Ezra, Nehemiah, Esther*, (Grand Rapids, MI: WM. B. Eerdmans Publishing Company, 1966), 306-307.

[3] Adam Clarke, LL.D., F.S.A., &c., *Clarke's Commentary*, vol. 2, *Joshua - Esther* (New York: Abingdon-Cokebury Press), 807.

[4] Jamieson, Fausset, Brown, 635.

[5] Clarke, 807.

[6] John Wesley Notes, *Power BibleCD*, (Bronson, MI: Online Publishing, Inc., 2003)

[7] Clarke, 807.

[8] Matthew Henry, *Commentary on the Whole Bible*, vol. 2, *Joshua-Esther*, (New York: Fleming H. Revell Company), 1123

[9] Jamieson, Fausset, Brown, 635.

[10] James Burton Cofman, *Coffman Commentary on Esther* - http://www.studylight.org

[11] Coffman

[12] Keil, Delitsch, 308.

[13] Clarke, 810.

[14] Clarke, 811.

[15] Clarke, 812-813.

[16] Jamieson, Fausset, Brown, 641.

[17] Ewen Montagu, *The Man Who Never Was*, (Philadelphia: J. B. Lippincott Company, 1954)

[18] Jamieson, Fausset, Brown, 644.

[19] Jamieson, Fausset, Brown, 648.

Made in the USA
Charleston, SC
07 August 2012